Pick up this book, read it, and tell me who can disagree with the thought of kindness being classy.

—Whoopi Goldberg

Candace's book shows that no matter how busy, overwhelmed, or hectic your life may be, there is *always* time to be kind.

—Jodie Sweetin

Candace has always been the epitome of kind and classy. We need more grace-filled women like Candace in this world.

—Kathie Lee Gifford

A book about niceness? Hey, you stole my idea!

—Joy Behar

This refreshingly positive read is a call to action for anyone who wants to live a more satisfying and fulfilling life. I'm in!

—Andrea Barber

Now more than ever we need to change the narrative in today's world. This is the perfect place to start.

—Lori Loughlin

In this book we are given a backstage pass to a counter-cultural, upside-down way of living and loving. Highly recommended!

—Karen Ehman, bestselling author;
Proverbs 31 Ministries speaker

This book reads like a letter from Candace to a friend, and that friend is *you!* Candace, thank you for sharing your faith walk and God's promises.

—Elisabeth Hasselbeck, @elisabethhasselbeck

I love how this book makes you evaluate areas in your life that need kindness in the center. This is an important book for the world we are living in.

—Korie Robertson

In this wonderful, wise, and practical book, Candace Cameron Bure gives a clear compelling vision of living a different way: firmly rooted in your convictions and also exceedingly gracious to others.

—David Kinnaman, author, *unChristian* and *Good Faith*; president, Barna

Candace's ability to put her finger on the pulse of what's relevant—and to show why it's important—is uncanny, and her recommendations make the world a better place.

—Bill Abbott, president and CEO, Hallmark Channel

These pages contain a refreshing message for women in our cultural moment. Candace exudes this beautifully. I'm grateful for this important book.

—Rebekah Lyons, author, *You Are Free* and *Freefall to Fly*

Candace brings virtue back to front and center where it has always belonged. This message of goodness couldn't be more timely.

—Gabe Lyons, president, Q; author, *Good Faith*

No one ever killed anyone with kindness—only the dark is killed by kindness. The rest of us are resurrected by it. Read with joy: you are holding a kind of resurrection in your hands.

—Ann Voskamp, bestselling author, *The Broken Way* and *One Thousand Gifts*

Kind is the New Classy

Kind is the New Classy

THE POWER OF LIVING GRACIOUSLY

CANDACE CAMERON BURE

With Ami McConnell

ZONDERVAN

ZONDERVAN

Kind Is the New Classy
Copyright © 2018 by Candache, Inc.

Requests for information should be addressed to:
Zondervan, 3900 *Sparks Dr. SE, Grand Rapids, Michigan 49546*

ISBN 978-0-310-35002-6 (hardcover)

ISBN 978-0-310-35395-9 (special edition)

ISBN 978-0-310-35164-1 (international trade paper edition)

ISBN 978-0-310-35229-7 (audio)

ISBN 978-0-310-35076-7 (ebook)

All Scripture quotations, unless otherwise indicated, are taken from the Holy Bible, New International Version®, NIV®. Copyright © 1973, 1978, 1984, 2011 by Biblica, Inc.® Used by permission of Zondervan. All rights reserved worldwide. www.Zondervan.com. The "NIV" and "New International Version" are trademarks registered in the United States Patent and Trademark Office by Biblica, Inc.®

Scripture quotations marked CSB® are taken from the Christian Standard Bible®, Copyright © 2017 by Holman Bible Publishers. Used by permission. Christian Standard Bible®, and CSB®, are federally registered trademarks of Holman Bible Publishers.

Scripture quotations marked ESV are taken from the ESV® Bible (The Holy Bible, English Standard Version®). Copyright © 2001 by Crossway, a publishing ministry of Good News Publishers. Used by permission. All rights reserved.

Scripture quotations marked MSG are taken from *The Message.* Copyright © by Eugene H. Peterson 1993, 1994, 1995, 1996, 2000, 2001, 2002. Used by permission of NavPress. All rights reserved. Represented by Tyndale House Publishers, Inc.

Scripture quotations marked NKJV are taken from the New King James Version®. © 1982 by Thomas Nelson. Used by permission. All rights reserved.

Scripture quotations marked NLT are taken from the Holy Bible, New Living Translation. © 1996, 2004, 2007, 2013, 2015 by Tyndale House Foundation. Used by permission of Tyndale House Publishers, Inc., Carol Stream, Illinois 60188. All rights reserved.

Any Internet addresses (websites, blogs, etc.) and telephone numbers in this book are offered as a resource. They are not intended in any way to be or imply an endorsement by Zondervan, nor does Zondervan vouch for the content of these sites and numbers for the life of this book.

Art direction: *Curt Diepenhorst*
Interior design: *Denise Froehlich*

First printing February 2018 / Printed in the United States of America

To my mom, Barbara, the epitome of kindness, compassion, love, and class. Thank you for being the best example of all. I love you.

Contents

Acknowledgments

A huge thank-you to my team for encouraging me to write a book not only based on my experiences but one that will prayerfully and hopefully change the mindset of every person who reads it to love more, respect more, value others more, and always keep it classy and kind. A special thank-you to Stephanie Smith for helping me formulate the big ideas as well as editing the small ones. Thank you Ami McConnell for your talent, teamwork, enthusiasm, prayers, and, most of all, patience with me. I know it wasn't easy! To Erin Davis for your willingness to dig in with me again, thank you.

There isn't anything in the last twenty years I have done without Ford Englerth and Jeffery Brooks. Your hard work and determination not only helped make my pursuit of my dreams come true but continued to push me to dream bigger and pray harder. I love you both up to the sky. Thank you Redrock Entertainment, my agents at Gersh, with special acknowledgment to Allison Cohen and attorney Chad Christopher. To James and Melissa at Anderson Group PR. To my biggest blessing since 2016, Snow White in the flesh, my other set of eyes, ears, hands, and brains, Bailey. I don't know how I ever did it without you.

Thank you to everyone at Zondervan for putting your heart and effort into this book. David Morris, Tom Dean, Brian Phipps, Robin Barnett, Jennifer VerHage, and Curt Diepenhorst. Many thanks for the beautiful cover shot by photographer Eric Michael Roy, makeup artist Tara Brooks, hairstylist Daniel Blaylock, and stylist Tara Williams.

Introduction

The Real Secret of

Classy Women

sat on the floor in the dark, knees pulled to my chest, face in my hands, sobbing. The three-by-two-foot closet of my dressing room at *The View* was the only place I could find to hide, work out my overwhelmed emotions, and pray to the Lord. I only hoped the closet door muffled the sound of my guttural cry, because I just couldn't keep it contained anymore.

I was about to go live on national television after hearing the reports of the San Bernardino terrorist attack after learning that fourteen people had been shot and killed and twenty-two others were seriously injured. The details were still coming in, and my cell phone kept ringing because Southern California schools had been put on lockdown, including the public middle and high schools my three kids attended. I felt so helpless, unable to protect my babies in Los Angeles from across the country in New York City. The heartbreak, disgust, and anger I was feeling had overtaken any sense of composure.

Moments before I crawled into my closet, I was in the bullpen getting details from the producers as the story unraveled, and I'd called my kids and finally reached Lev on his cell.

The bullpen is what we call the open-plan office area where all the producers, writers, and their assistants work at their desks, making morning-of-show decisions, tracking the current news, and gathering research materials the cohosts may need to prove their point. Just like the area where pitchers go to warm up during a game, this area is crowded, chaotic, and often tense before a live show.

"Are you okay? Do you feel safe? Tell me how you're feeling," I asked. After a brief chat, we hung up and I called my husband, Val, who had been filling me in on school details. When he heard the questions I'd asked Lev, he got upset.

"Why would you play into the fear? Why didn't you reassure him everything *is* okay and they aren't in any danger? You're causing panic that was never there for them."

I was speechless. How could my questions of concern to my children be overshadowed by Val's concern that I'd said the wrong things to them? My emotions got hot and heated, which isn't typical for me unless I'm on the brink of overload. I raised my voice in anger and started crying uncontrollably. Despite my attempts to keep my cool and lower my voice, I'm sure everyone could hear me.

That's when I did what I've seen my daughter do when she's upset and wants to be alone. I hung up the phone and hid in the tiny closet in my dressing room. Tears streamed down my face as I tried to calm myself and figure out how to pull it together enough to get through the live, one-hour show that started in just thirty minutes.

That's when I heard a knock on my dressing room door. I didn't want to talk to anyone, and I hadn't caught my breath enough to do so anyway, so I ignored it. But the knock persisted. I waited, hoping whoever it was would go away. They knocked again. I slowly opened the closet door and stood up, wiped the tears from my face, and took a deep breath. "Maybe they'll leave," I thought. But louder and firmer, the knocking continued. So I opened the dressing room door, and there stood my cohost, Whoopi Goldberg.

"May I come in?" she asked gently.

"Yes," I managed to whisper.

She took a step into my dressing room and closed the door behind her. There she stood with open arms as she said, "Come here." She hugged me, like a mama bear hugs and protects her babies. I sobbed into her shoulder, knowing I was probably getting her crisp white shirt smeared with mascara. She didn't care about the shirt. She kept hugging me until I decided to let go.

"You're gonna be fine," she said. "I've got your back. I won't let you fall out there. It's gonna be okay. Just speak from your heart today."

That simple act of kindness was more valuable to me than any extravagant present. It was genuine kindness, pure and simple. Whoopi saw me in distress, and she offered compassion and protection, not because she owed it to me or because it would bring her personal gain but simply as a selfless act. She put herself in my shoes and offered exactly what she would have wanted in that moment if our roles had been reversed. Because of that moment of kindness, I was able to walk onto the set with a little more hope that day, just when I needed it most.

What Money Can't Buy

Picture Audrey Hepburn with her hair swept high behind a jeweled tiara, wearing big black sunglasses, in a classic little black dress. Maybe, like me, you think of her in *Breakfast at Tiffany's*—with her diamond choker necklace and long satin gloves—as the ultimate image of *classy*.

Or maybe you think of elegant and prestigious hotels like the Plaza in New York City, or those perfume ads with stunning stars like Charlize Theron or Natalie Portman dressed in gorgeous gowns, surrounded by roses. When I say classy, maybe you think of black-tie affairs, strings of pearls, or striking high heels.

While those images certainly feel classy, I believe that true classiness comes from the heart, in the form of kindness. Because no matter what you're wearing, what you're driving, where you're staying, or how much cash you have in the bank, kindness never goes out of style, and it makes all the difference in the world.

Every day, in a hundred ways, women encounter ads trying to sell us things that promise to make us look and feel amazing. I've bought my fair share of face creams, shapewear, and juice cleanses, I freely admit! But the things that make a woman feel good inside and out—and make those around her feel good and happy to be with her—are not for sale. Things like kindness, self-discipline, purpose, humility, grace, confidence, hospitality, and peace cannot be marketed in a slick magazine ad or in a movie.

That's why I wanted to write this book. I believe our world is in need of more women who value the virtue of kindness. I hope this book will be a soul-inspiring invitation to you to embody gracefulness in moments big and small. Sure, it's gonna take some effort. Kindness doesn't come easy, because it goes against the grain of our me-first mentality. But it will be so worth it, and frankly the stakes are sky-high if we don't.

We live in a unique moment in time. I'm so grateful for the trailblazing women who've gone before me—the ones who carved the path that you and I walk now. Women like Marie Curie, Rosa Parks, Emmeline Pankhurst, Jeannette Rankin, Gertrude Ederle, Amelia Earhart, Harriet Beecher Stowe, Billie Jean King, Valentina Tereshkova, and Lucille Ball, to name a few. These women pushed boundaries for the good of others, redefining what women can and can't do, and setting some seriously classy examples for us all.

When I was growing up, my parents encouraged each of us kids—my brother, two sisters, and me—to pursue our passions. If we had a goal, they helped guide us and support us to achieve it. Gender was never considered a true barrier in our house. That wasn't the case when my mom or my grandmothers were growing up, but it was for me and my sisters. Thanks to our parents' support, we knew that if we put our minds to it, we could do anything.

Never before have women had the freedoms we have today. And choices? We have choices in abundance! My daughter Natasha recently graduated from high school. As we've walked through this season of transition together, I've told her often that she has the power to choose exactly what her life looks like from here on out. The world is truly her oyster, and there are pearls everywhere she looks. What would women even fifty years ago have given to have so many choices?

Granted, we each have limitations. But for American women with strong resolve, nothing is off the table. We have more opportunities than we've ever had before.

Of course, there is a flip side to this thrilling freedom. The Bible teaches, "From everyone who has been given much, much will be demanded" (Luke 12:48). Or, as Spider-Man's Uncle Ben Parker spins it, "With great power comes great responsibility." (Don't you love it when Hollywood unknowingly teaches biblical truth?)

I believe our responsibility is to love each other just as

God has loved us. As Christians, we are called to live out Christ's example of love to a watching world, and love in action is simply kindness. Of course there will be differences and disagreements. But no matter what clashes come your way, I've found that kindness always wins the day.

And I think we could all use some more of that.

The Fear Effect

Though gifted with tremendous freedom, American women can be a fearful bunch. I know because I experience this too. We fear we're not parenting our children the right way. We fear our efforts won't be enough and will fail those around us. We fear that we aren't keeping up with the Joneses or keeping our bodies in good shape or that our iniquities may get exposed in broad daylight. We fear we may lose our rights, and we fear the uncertainty of the world we live in. I guess it's human nature to want to hold on to what you have—to not lose control. But I have to ask myself, "Is shouting, posting negative hot takes on social media, and generally working up a good froth of anger going to make things better long-term? Are anger and bitterness and fear the tools we can really use to build a better world?"

Don't get me wrong; there's a place for righteous anger. Jesus himself went into the temple and turned over the tables in frustration. In John 11, we read that when His friend Lazarus died, Jesus was "deeply troubled" and "deep anger welled up within him" (v. 33 NLT), but my hunch is that most of our angry outbursts just breed more frustration instead of lasting change.

We live in an outrage culture. We are so quick to lash out at those we disagree with, to get riled up about the latest hot take. But what if we decided to turn the tables and work toward a *kindness culture* instead?

To do that, we have to first contend with our own fear. Because if you ask me, behind every reactionary tweet, text, or retort is a very real fear at work.

I'm an optimist. I don't think we can hold on to something good by being anxious and fearful about it. That's one lesson my faith has taught me. Fear keeps us spinning our wheels, stuck in the lie that we can't do anything to make a difference. What we *can* do is create a better world by each choosing to be better people, consciously becoming more and more like Jesus, who is Love and Kindness in the flesh. We can impact others by being conduits of God's tremendous grace. When we do, His grace can fill up the space between us created by disagreements on cultural issues and relational tension.

Can you imagine what the world would look like if more of us resolved to live as kind, classy, confident women instead of women "empowered" by the idea that the world owes us something? We need God's help to flip a switch in our hearts. What we want to be is "in-powered" by the Holy Spirit, because there are no mountains God cannot move.

An empowered woman believes she can do anything because her own strength, courage, boldness, and drive are enough. An in-powered woman believes she can do anything because God is enough. God holds all those attributes and more and supplies them to every one of us, even when we don't think we're capable of carrying them.

The Real Secret to Culture Change

In this book, we'll talk about character traits I believe make women truly remarkable. You can't buy them for any amount of money, but their value is greater than we could ever imagine! In my faith walk, we sometimes refer to these virtues as the fruit of the Spirit: love, joy, peace, patience, kindness, goodness, faithfulness, gentleness, and self-control (Gal. 5:22–23 ESV). These characteristics come from God's Spirit alive in the human heart. These qualities are not specially reserved for the elite few; rather I believe any woman can cultivate these characteristics. It simply takes choice and lifelong practice.

So I've written this book for those of us who want to change our culture by changing ourselves, one woman at a time.

Think about it this way. A me-first mentality is normalized in our culture, and it often results in rudeness toward others.

Gossiping behind someone else's back is the norm.

Snubbing a person on social media is the norm.

Taking credit for another's hard work is the norm.

We see this me-first mentality at work every time we get cut off in traffic, snapped at in conversation, or put down so that someone else can prop themselves up. And we can all find glimpses of the me-first mentality in the mirror if we take a good look.

But friends, will you imagine with me for a moment? Sure, it's normal and human nature to be generally inconsiderate of others. But what if we started being radically considerate to each other instead? What if, instead of living me-first, we embarked on an experiment to first consider others?

This is the essence of kindness. Character is countercultural. So let's clear the deck right now of any misconception that kindness is just the stuff of sentimental greeting cards. No, it's the stuff of culture change. It's the stuff of revival.

Kindness is incredibly powerful because it is so unlike what most of us see every day. It does not come naturally to us. We have to work at it and build it, like a muscle. But when we do, it stands out.

The me-first mentality only looks to climb the social ladder; kindness treats everyone equally.

The me-first mentality walks into a room asking what it can get; kindness walks into a room seeking to give with no expectation of return.

The me-first mentality sizes people up according to outward appearance; kindness sees each and every person as precious and uniquely crafted in the image of God.

Are you starting to see it yet? In a world where rudeness and selfishness is the norm, a simple act of kindness can spark radical change. It's classy, it's countercultural, and it stands to make a world of difference.

Are you in?

The Best Example

Years ago, I made a decision to serve Jesus with every aspect of my life. So I often think, "What will people say about Jesus because of me?" In both the entertainment industry and my personal life, this question really motivates me. And no one better exemplifies kindness than Him.

As I study the Bible, I marvel at how Jesus affected those around Him. He went out of His way to make people feel truly seen and loved. He treated everyone with equal dignity, regardless of their social status, wealth, education, or gender. And He sought to serve not only His friends but strangers too, and even His enemies—the test of any true kindness.

Jesus was once asked what the greatest commandment is that people should follow. I just love His response: "'Love the Lord your God with all your heart and with all your soul and with all your mind and with all your strength.'

The [second-greatest commandment] is this: 'Love your neighbor as yourself.' There is no commandment greater than these" (Mark 12:30–31).

Life has gotten so complicated. We all feel this as we look at our calendars, our budgets, our phones, and the demands of keeping up in a fast-moving world. Yet kindness gets us back to the basics.

That's what I see in Jesus' words here: love reigns most important of all.

People think success in life will make them happy. But it's kindness, which connects us to others, that makes life meaningful.

Our society is bent to be transactional. But kindness bucks all the rules and says, "Even though I have nothing to gain from you, I care about you. Even though you have no social capital to offer me, I want to give you a gift." It doesn't matter whether someone is a janitor or the prime minister. Kindness isn't looking to climb the social ladder, win a debate, or gain something from the relationship. Rather kindness seeks to *give*—without thought or condition of return. A one-size-fits-all policy toward all people, in the recognition that all people are made in the image of God.

When we live in a me-first mentality, we get stuck in the small world of our individuality. Yet when we practice putting others first, following Christ's example, that small world expands. We find that we are connected with others, that we do not walk through this uncertain world alone. We find that God shows up in everyday actions.

Jesus was a kindness champion. And I hope to follow His lead.

Party Pooper

Now let me ask you, do you consider yourself kind and classy? Maybe you've recently said or done something that made you feel ashamed, like you're the opposite of kind. If that's you, believe me, I struggle with this too. In fact, let me tell you a story.

It was my thirty-eighth birthday, and I'd just competed on week 4 of *Dancing with the Stars*. My best friend, Dilini, had planned a big birthday bash for me after the show, at a nearby swanky LA hotel. Friends, family, coworkers, and fellow contestants and dancers from the show were all in attendance to celebrate with great food, drinks, custom desserts, and a fun photo booth. Quiet, mellow music was playing in the background, but it wasn't dancing music, and what I really wanted was a DJ. But the indoor-outdoor space we were in was too close to the restaurant, so they didn't allow additional music. I was disappointed because I really wanted to dance. It's my thing! Not that I'm great at it, but dancing with wild abandon is one of my most freeing and fun things to do. I immediately complained to my BFF and begged the managers to allow us to change the music so we could dance. They said they'd see what they could do, but to no avail. The music wasn't changing, and we weren't going to have a dance party. I was upset and wouldn't shake it off.

For the most part, I allowed my irritation to cloud the celebration. I couldn't seem to get over it and continued to pout, thinking how terrible the party was for everyone without the right music. I kept thinking that if only *I* had planned the party, I wouldn't have let that be an oversight, and if I had taken control, it would have been perfect. And I wasn't afraid to let my best friend know it. Okay, I'll just say what I know you're already thinking: I was the most ungrateful person ever. I'm not proud of it, but in that moment, an ugliness came out in me I didn't realize existed.

I woke up the next morning with a terrible feeling in my gut. I was sick to my stomach and knew exactly the reason why. I picked up the phone and dialed Dilini's number. "Hi. Before you say anything, please let me talk. I. Am. So. Sorry." I went on to apologize from the depths of my soul, asking for her forgiveness and grace. After I ate as much humble pie as I could possibly stomach, she said to me, "I'm glad you said what you did. You know I hate confrontation, and we've never fought before. But if you hadn't started off the conversation this way and apologized without me asking you to, something was going to change in our twenty-two-year relationship forever!"

Dilini forgave me, and I vowed to never take out my unrelated stress and project it onto her or anyone else like that again. I certainly didn't feel kind or classy in that moment. I felt like a jerk.

But Dilini exemplified kindness to me in that moment. She inspired me by living out what I believe is the essence of kindness—remaining kind to me even when I was unkind to her. And I hope her example, as well as many others in this book, will inspire you too. I believe we can all learn how to grow in the characteristics we'll talk about in this book. And together we're going to grow toward changing our world from the inside out. So let's get started!

CHAPTER 1

Finding "Your "Why"

Kindness knows its purpose

Not a day goes by that I'm not thankful for the amazing job I have. I get to entertain people through comedy, romance, drama, and heartfelt storytelling by acting my way through your television screens.

Maybe you watched me grow up in front of your eyes or alongside you on *Full House*, but today my work is so much more than that. For the last three years (so far), I've filled the shoes of DJ Tanner once again on Netflix's *Fuller House*, going to work every weekday at Warner Brothers Studios in Burbank, California, to film new weekly episodes. I get to laugh and play with my costars, who happen to be some of my best friends, and act my heart out alongside them.

But don't let all the comedy fool you. My days consist of learning ever-changing dialogue, rehearsals which often involve major physical performances, wardrobe fittings, time in hair and makeup (which isn't as fun as it sounds when you do it every day), and pretaping every scene in advance of our live audience shows every Friday night. Do that for twenty-five weeks straight, and it becomes pretty exhausting.

During my hiatus, when I'm not working on *Fuller*

House, I'm off to Vancouver or various North American cities to film movies for the Hallmark Channel and my movie series on the Hallmark Movies and Mysteries channel, the Aurora Teagarden Mysteries, which I also executive produce. Each of those films takes approximately three weeks to shoot, but that doesn't include the weeks for preproduction and postproduction, which means putting the movie together through locations, hiring the cast and crew, editing, sound, music, technical special effects, and more. While I don't personally do all those jobs, I oversee the process and make decisions to ensure I'm producing the best project I can for the network and viewers.

In between my "day job" as an actor and producer, I work hard to squeeze in time to write books, develop more television and movie projects, design products, and speak at women's conferences. I also have to be available for press, media, and book tours to promote each of these projects. To say I'm an overachiever may be an understatement. My work is both rewarding and demanding! Admittedly, it has its downsides, but honestly, I wake up every morning and thank God I get to work with incredibly talented people creating something that will enrich people's lives and entertain them. It's truly a dream come true!

Unlike most jobs, my work comes along in spurts rather than a predictable nine to five. It's feast or famine, and lately I've been in a season of feast. I know all too well that can turn on a dime.

The entertainment industry capitalizes on who's hot at the moment, which can come for a variety of reasons: talent, ratings in terms of dollar figures, a large fan base, the nostalgia factor, personal relationships, or headline potential (good or bad), just to name a few! On the flip side of the same coin, the industry also tells you when they've moved on and think your time is up, despite your resume. After a couple of misses, a few failed TV pilots, or just never being quite right for a lead role, many actors seem to disappear as if they chose to leave, when in reality many of them aren't being hired in place of who "they" think is the next best thing.

Age, race, and gender also play a significant role in the entertainment business. There are ages, particularly for women, that don't have as many written roles. In 2016 and 2017, across all platforms such as cable, streaming, and broadcast networks, female actors comprised 42 percent of all speaking characters, with only 28 percent of women in behind-the-camera positions such as creators, directors, writers, producers, executive producers, editors, and directors of photography.[1] (The very reason you see a trend from the women in Hollywood speaking out to have more options and more available roles.) A woman in her forties, like me, typically works less than a woman in her late twenties to late thirties, because we've surpassed the

....

1   *http://womenandhollywood.com/resources/statistics/tv-statistics/.*

wedding and new mom phase and aren't quite the age of grandparents. And unless you've become an A-list star, the older you get, the less options there are.

Of course, there are several working actors who have maintained steady careers for decades, and I attribute the majority of that to their talent, perseverance, love for their craft, or good reputation. The unknown is the constant in my career, no matter how successful you think you are, and frankly it's a bit scary. I trust God to provide, but I'd be lying if I said I never thought about when the next season of famine will come my way.

Still, sometimes roles, projects, and companies come along that I must say no to. Just recently I was wrapping up a project in Vancouver when my phone pinged. A new script had been delivered via email, with a title that grabbed my attention. I got excited because I love to read great stories, crafted by talented writers who draw me in and capture my imagination. But as I dove into the script later that night, I realized with a sinking feeling that this was not a story I was willing to help tell. When a script is not edifying or doesn't have a hopeful or redemptive message or makes me feel uncomfortable, my conscience won't let me take on that role. Sure, saying yes might bring me success according to the world's definition—money, fame, exposure—but that's not enough to persuade me. I'm motivated by staying true to my values and convictions. Sometimes I pass on a project, like this particular script, knowing that future offers may not come back around. But I know this is ultimately a better choice than starring in something I don't believe in.

You've probably faced similar pressures in your life. The world has a habit of defining us if we don't know who we are before we get out there. When an exciting opportunity comes our way, we can be tempted to edit ourselves in ways large and small so we'll fit the role the world wants us to fill. It's easy to look at compromise and think, "That's not too terrible of a cost, right?" To get the job, to fit in with the right people, to make the dream come to life. This can make us feel like we're being pulled in a million directions, *trying* to live for the right thing but unsure what that is. That's why it's so important to know your purpose with clarity and conviction before you're ever in a situation of compromise.

The Difference between Primary Purpose and Secondary Priorities

Everything I set out to do is for the glory of God. That's my purpose in life. My other priorities—staying fit and healthy, working hard and growing in my career in the entertainment business, raising a healthy, happy family— all are in service to this higher purpose.

When I'm making a choice, I get to weigh each decision in light of whether it will further my *true* purpose. I used the phrase "I get to" intentionally. Knowing my purpose is a huge blessing! It's like having a built-in compass when the people around you are looking to a cloudy sky to try to find true north. Taking the role I mentioned earlier would *not* have been in line with my purpose, even if it could have helped boost my career. Ultimately, any career progress would have been meaningless because it would have undermined my objective to glorify God.

Because of this compass, success and failure are redefined in my life. Goals have outcomes others may not see as valuable. The work I do may not always seem as successful to the critics. None of that changes my decisions, because my purpose remains the same. As I seek His glory first, each outcome prepares me for the next season.

I haven't always had this clarity of purpose guiding my life and choices. There's no doubt I had a great foundation of priorities growing up. My parents insisted that we lived by high moral principles. I'm so grateful for all that they invested in me. They taught me so much. Come to think of it, they're still teaching me with the way they live and love, but my own faith walk really began when my kids were very young.

I'd been working steadily in the entertainment industry for fifteen years when I married the love of my life, Val Bure, a professional hockey player. Val and I determined when we married that we wanted to have one parent at home while we raised our family. Val would retire from hockey at some point, so I decided to be home with the kids when they were little.

But the decision didn't come easily. I was at peace in that I felt a conviction to stay home with my kids; however, the first few years weren't as glorious and joyful as I expected them to be. It was a tough transition, going from full-time work from age five to twenty-one to full-time stay-at-home mom. I had gone from traveling, working with new people in new places every year, and being in the Hollywood spotlight to being at home all day long with my infant and toddler while my husband was at work. My world had grown smaller. There were no directors or producers to glorify my achievements. Instead I was changing diapers, doing the laundry, cleaning the house, wiping up spit-up and dog slobber, taking walks to the park and doing anything else that would get me out of the house, only for the glory of waking up and doing it all over again. No "Well done, Candace!" No awards. Just me, my kids, and my hubby, when he was in town.

At the time, I couldn't clearly see my purpose. I'd often think, "Is this really going to be the rest of my life? Giving it all up? Will I ever get *me* back?" As a young working woman, I had only thought about myself. Now, as a young wife and mom, I had to put aside self and put others first. Easier said than done when you're not used to it. But we had three beautiful, active children by 2002: Natasha, Lev, and Maksim. As I looked at their adorable faces around my breakfast table each morning, I wondered,

"How am I going to raise these precious children?"

"What do I believe, really?"

"What do I want *them* to believe?"

I began to search the Bible—God's Word—and pray like never before. After some serious soul-searching, the gospel message became clear to me. I was in my midtwenties with three small children constantly at my feet when I decided to put my faith first. Being a mother helped me see that I wanted to live for God.

What a paradigm shift! For the first time, my relationship with God became my primary focus, instead of my career. That decision changed every level and every layer of my life. Yes, I do have a successful career now, but I didn't pursue a relationship with God in order to be successful. I wanted to know God and to understand *His* purpose for my life. Through prayer and God's Word, I felt like I knew what God had for me. He was saying, "I've prepared you, and now you have a fresh set of eyes to see what you're here for. It's to be a good representation of my people and the good things I have in store for everyone."

Deciding to put God first in my life is one of the riskiest things I've ever done. Trust me, if you're trying to make it in Hollywood, coming out as a Christian isn't the best way to do it! My managers and I laugh about this all the time. It's so counterintuitive. But I knew it was right for me.

Many people in the entertainment industry wrote me off and said I'd never work again if I took some time off to raise my children. But having one parent in the home was important to Val and me, and it was during those years when my kids were small that my faith really took root. Those roots hold me steady to this day.

Setting Your Life's GPS

Spend a few minutes surfing social media, and you'll quickly discover that we love to talk about purpose. The messages of destiny, dreaming big, and finding what you were born for are woven throughout American culture.

But I'm not talking about some pie-in-the-sky purpose with no application in our everyday lives. I'm simply addressing the reason I exist, my motivation for the decisions I must make in my daily life, from the big stuff like "Where will we live?" "How many kids will we have?" "What kind of work will I pursue?" to the seemingly small stuff like "What will I eat?" "How will I spend this window of free time?" "What will I say?"

It's my experience that most women aren't living for the *wrong* purpose exactly; they just haven't given much thought to their purpose at all. I would say this was once my experience. In fact, by not knowing my ultimate purpose, I felt pulled in a million directions by many secondary purposes, so much so that I felt spread thin. It was hard to know where to direct my attention at any given time and how to prioritize my energy, between the demands of my career, commitment to family, friendships, personal health, and more.

Those years when I was at home with my small children worked like a greenhouse, helping me grow my understanding of what my *primary* purpose is, beyond any other ambitions in life. If you'd asked me my purpose before those years, I would have fumbled to find an answer. Now I know.

My purpose is to glorify God.

With so many voices and influences seeking to define our purpose for us, it's easy to get confused. The world hands us so many scripts. We are told to be perfect in so many ways. To be successful, confident, beautiful, all-star parents, wives, daughters, teachers, and role models.

Often we put the cart before the horse, seeing the specific *ways* we live out our purpose as the purpose itself.

Being a champion for the poor, fighting human trafficking, or helping the sick are worthy and valuable causes, but they are not our ultimate purpose. They are simply the means to glorify God by caring for others. Bringing God glory is the *purpose*; the specific ways we do that are the *process*.

Acting, writing, speaking, mothering—none of these are my primary purpose. They are the roles God has given me to live out my higher purpose of glorifying Him. If I looked to any one of those roles to give my life meaning, I'd struggle when things in that single area didn't go well. But since I know my purpose is to bring God glory, I have freedom to live it out in every area of my life. I am even free to fail, because it's possible to glorify God through my weaknesses.

Often we get clues about our purpose through our passions. You may be passionate about music or teaching or gathering people in your home. That's great! Think of your passions as road markers on the map that help you take steps toward your purpose. Purpose is the reason we exist, and it can help us set the GPS for our lives.

Was It Nuts?

Looking back at my life, I have to laugh at God's providence. The entertainment industry said I was nuts to take time off to be at home to raise my kids. It's difficult enough for a child actor to transition into an adult actor, and when *Full House* ended, I was at the prime age for the transition to take place. When you're on a roll, like being on a successful television show, you don't leave the industry. You're told to ride the wave, move with your momentum into a new light, with new roles taking you into the next phase of your career. If you stop for college or for family, you might be forgotten. How many successful child actors can you think of who came back as successful adult actors? There are just a handful of names that span decades in the industry.

But making my family a priority is a decision I've never regretted. Not even for an instant. I look back at that time, when I was home with my babies, with wonder and awe. It wasn't easy. Far from it! It takes a lot of work, a lot of patience, and constant help from God and His Word to be a parent. But we made it. I'm so grateful God helped me raise confident, thriving kids.

To be honest, while I was at home full-time, I often wrestled with not working. Even though I had willfully and joyfully surrendered to motherhood a few years into that season of life, I was always hopeful that I would go back into the entertainment industry at some point. For so long, my identity had been tied up in my work as an actress.

I remember being in the grocery store, seven months pregnant, when the butcher behind the deli counter recognized me as I asked for a half pound of sliced turkey. He told me how much he loved *Full House* and that his kids watched it all the time. I could see his excitement over encountering me in person.

He asked me what movies I was currently working on, and I said, "None. I'm going to have a baby!" It was then that the brightness left his face. He cast his eyes down, said, "Oh," and busied himself working on my order.

I couldn't tell whether he was sad because I wasn't

acting anymore or because he thought I was an unwed (my fingers were too swollen to wear my wedding ring), pregnant teenager (because I still looked like one at twenty-one) who stumbled down the wrong path as a child star. I walked away feeling disappointed, worthless, and embarrassed.

The same question from fans everywhere I went was a constant reminder that my value and identity was in my work. Would people still care about me if wasn't acting anymore? Would they still meet me with the same enthusiasm knowing I was just a normal person like them? When I wasn't in that role anymore, I couldn't help but wonder who I was and what I was about. As I wrestled, I began to understand that my worth isn't defined by what I do. That insight didn't come overnight, of course, but over time I resolved in my heart that it would be okay if I didn't work again. My faith in God assures me that my worth isn't determined by the applause of others or by my achievements. Through His Word, God says to me, "No matter what, you're loved, you're precious, and you're mine." That clarity of *whose* I am is so helpful for me!

I think of it this way: Are my kids less precious to me when they fail than when they succeed? No way! I love them simply because they're mine. That's how it is with God. He is our Father, and He's the best Father you could ask for, because He. Is. Love. (See 1 John 4:8.) Nothing I can do will make Him love me any more or any less. He loves me simply because I am His. What an amazing gift that has been to me, a gift I'm still opening daily.

When Val retired from hockey, we decided to prioritize my career for the next season of our life together. He would be at home with the kids while I pursued my acting career again in earnest. That's when I was offered a role on the series *Make It or Break It*. It turns out Val is actually a better "mom" than I ever was! He's a much better cook, is always on top of our schedules, and is rarely ruffled even amid the daily demands of parenthood.

Did my career suffer from that self-enforced break from the business? If so, I haven't noticed. When I take the long view, I can easily see that those years raising my family and getting to know God were well spent and extremely fruitful. I wouldn't change a thing. And I'm so grateful that by the time I returned to my work, I was rooted in my purpose and able to look to this as my true compass for whatever came next.

Trusting in the "Foolishness" of God

The world said I was crazy then. Now the world says I'm nuts to be candid about my faith. If you follow me on social media, you've seen this dialogue come up a lot. Not everyone appreciates a woman who is outspoken about her faith, but I'm not too worried. With clarity of purpose, such external expectations don't rock you. Of course, that doesn't mean life isn't full of surprises. And it doesn't mean others won't see this as controversial.

So when *The View* asked me to come aboard as a cohost, I was shocked. I had always been an actress with a script to memorize and speak from. What did I know about being a talk show host? As I considered the offer, I knew I'd be called upon to speak about current events every day. And given my beliefs, I knew my opinion would often be at odds with the views of others on the panel.

But I trusted that God had paved the way for me to be on that show. I knew my purpose, and it seemed to me that if He was opening this door, I needed to step through it. After much prayer and seeking out the advice of those who know me best, I decided to take the leap and accepted the job. I'll share more about that season as we go, but for now know that God made each step clear to me, allowing me a greater platform than I'd had before. Women from all over tell me that seeing me speak up about my beliefs on *The View* has emboldened them to speak up for their own beliefs. Their stories inspire me, giving me fuel for the next leg of my journey.

Finding Your Why

Women who clearly feel good in their own skin have a light that shines from within. That light makes you want to know what they're about. As I find these women and start asking questions, time after time I discover that such women have the same strong sense of purpose, the same sense of true north we've been talking about. For such women, it's not about their own vanity or ego; these women are outwardly focused. I like what Viktor E. Frankl wrote in the classic book *Man's Search for Meaning*: "Those who have a 'why' to live, can bear with almost any 'how.'"

Women who know the *why* of their existence can figure out *how* to live it out with grace and tenacity.

You may have read about my dear friend Mandy Young in my other books. She's a certified medical phenomenon, having a gene mutation technically named IRAK4 Gene Defect. Incredibly, her body forms its own recurring severe infections, putting her at constant risk. Mandy has had this life-threatening disease her whole life. Through complications from it, she lost her leg at the tender age of nine. She's been hospitalized more times than she can count, but she radiates joy and gratitude.

She lives this sort of purpose-driven life I want for each of us. Her life is a radiant prism. Her purpose is like a light that catches the eye of everyone she meets. She says, "I have led a life that most might not find enjoyable, but I love my life and I wouldn't change a thing. God has truly blessed me. I sometimes just have to remind myself that God only gives me what I can handle and that what doesn't kill me will only make me stronger."

When we know our why, it can anchor us through any

storm. And it can help us discern between our primary purpose and our secondary priorities. So the next time the world sends the wrong script your way, you'll be equipped to stay true to God's purpose and plan for you.

Purpose Doesn't Make Life Easier, Just Better

Living for a higher purpose nudges us to be the best version of ourselves. Though you'd think putting yourself second this way would drain your energy, it actually does the opposite: it *gives* you energy when, without such a purpose, you might find yourself depleted, discouraged, or adrift.

Val and I think it's incredibly important to give back to others. We look for opportunities to serve, especially together as a family. Several years ago, we decided to join our friends and take our kids to spend Christmas morning at a homeless shelter. We brought all the fixin's and cooked a breakfast feast for thirty to forty people, then sat down and ate with them. We talked, we listened, we laughed, shed some tears, and sang Christmas carols. We also shared the gospel message. Afterward we were so energized! Since then we've made it an annual tradition. While you might not look forward to serving, you'll find that once you've done it, it's not costly; it's a gift. Walking in step with your higher purpose is an indescribable blessing.

Not There Yet

Maybe you're reading this and nodding your head in agreement. I hope you're feeling firm in your conviction about your purpose. Even so, you may have a nagging frustration that you're not quite yet the sort of kind and classy woman you want to be. However you're feeling, hear me in this: God is preparing you right now, even if you're in a tough season.

Jesus said it this way: "In this world you will have trouble. But take heart! I have overcome the world" (John 16:33).

This assurance makes me smile every time. The pressure is off, sisters! He's already done the hard work. We just need to keep putting one foot in front of the other to accomplish the task He has set before us, with our eyes set on the prize of living our lives for His glory. Believe me, keeping your eyes lifted to your higher purpose works! I've been looking in God's direction for a long time now and have never ever regretted it.

If your goal is to have little angels for children, an immaculate and picture-perfect home, a successful, high-paying career, a hundred thousand followers on Instagram, and a bikini-ready body, I urge you to rethink. These are scripts that will lead us astray. You'll never live up to your own expectations, someone will always outdo you, and you will eventually feel defeated. Have you noticed that living for ourselves may feel good in a brief moment but always makes us feel miserable in the end? We find fulfillment and joy when we look up from our own navels.

"What's Different about Her?"

I feel passionately about taking time to define your purpose, because our culture will try to do it for you if you don't get there first. The voices of media and marketing will always be shouting loudly about how you should live and who you should live for. People will try to hand you new scripts every day.

The world does not expect successful women to put their careers on hold to raise the kids.

Or to have joy when facing a life-threatening illness.

Or to speak out about their faith when it's not popular.

Or to turn down opportunities without knowing what's to come.

Or to burn time and energy serving others' needs instead of their own.

But when you have a strong sense of purpose, the clarity and meaning will give you strength. That strength will radiate from you like a light. People around you will begin to ask, "What is it about you that makes you different?"

Your Turn

Some of you might be thinking, "But what if I'm not clear on my purpose? How can I figure it out?"

Schedule a Saturday morning, make yourself a nice pot of coffee, and give yourself the gift of time to dig in and find clarity. It will likely take some elbow grease and a reshuffling of your priorities, but it is worth it, for you and for those around you. Life will still be challenging, but it will not be aimless. Knowing your purpose helps you define your destination. And it sets the GPS for your life, guiding you through daily decisions, big and small, to help you get there.

Here are some ideas that have worked for me.

- **LOOK FOR CUES IN YOUR PAST.** What motivated you in the past? What in your life have you seen as being most worthy of your time and energy? Are there lessons you learned about what your purpose is *not?*

- **CONSIDER YOUR PASSIONS IN THE PRESENT.** What gets you excited? What do you love to talk about? What gifts do you feel God has given you? Do these passions point to something bigger than you?

- **PRAY TO THE PURPOSE MAKER.** I'm a big advocate of prayer! You can write out what you want to say to God on paper or on your phone. You can pray out loud while pushing your baby in a stroller or pray silently on your knees. Ask God to reveal your purpose. Give it time. He will be faithful!

- **LISTEN.** Be quiet and attentive to what God may be saying to you in this time. Even little signs can be helpful, so take note and write them down when you can to figure out what God may be trying to tell you. And ask for observations from those who know and love you. Poll friends and family by asking them questions about what gifts and passions they see in you, and listen to their answers carefully.

- **JOURNAL.** Writing is helpful for me and has been for a good portion of my life. I especially like to write down my prayers so I can see what I talked about with God and remember the many prayers He has already answered. When I flip through my journals, sometimes I read about what I struggled with in the past, and I can see His faithfulness in the answers. Sometimes the trivial stuff just gets worked out there on the page, and I find I can focus on what matters most to me.

CHAPTER 2

Grace under Fire

Kindness keeps its cool
even in the hot topics

Who knew a T-shirt could cause so much controversy?

It was a spring day on the set of *Fuller House*. I had just gone through makeup and hair in preparation for our pretape day. I hadn't gotten into wardrobe yet, so I was dressed casually in my own clothes. I wore sweatpants and a T-shirt that said, "Not today, Satan"—a shirt I'd ordered on Amazon just days before, when a friend showed it to me online. We both loved it and had to have it.

I wore it the day after it arrived in the mail. I guess you could say I needed an extra boost of confidence from God, a reminder that He had my back. Bouts of depression and anxiety had crept into mind and body in 2016; it was something I hadn't experienced since my early twenties. Like many people, it's easy for me to get overwhelmed juggling work, travel, and family commitments. But there comes a point when the overwhelm crosses into something deeper. Things I used to seamlessly multitask had started to overcome me with exhaustion, stress, panic, and depression.

And so, thinking about my work deadlines, my to-do list for the weekend, and my need to be present, focused, and available for my family began to make my heart beat fast. I grabbed hold of my T-shirt and told myself, "Nope, not today, Satan."

It reminded me that even when I'm not feeling strong enough to handle the attacks of the Enemy, God is always able. It was, for me, a personal declaration of what Scripture says more eloquently: "I can do all things through Christ who strengthens me" (Phil. 4:13 NKJV). It was my small way of taking a stand and declaring the powerful truth that God protects me from Satan.

I posted a picture of me wearing this shirt on my Instagram account because I thought it would encourage people in my social media feed. I was right; thousands of people commented, energized by it. Their support encouraged me and brought me extra joy.

All I knew was that "Not today, Satan" means something to me. Jesus rebuked Satan, and in Jesus' name we can do the same. What an incredible promise to stand on. As I pulled my T-shirt over my head that morning, I felt I was putting on the armor of God. It made me feel confident, protected, and ready to kick-start a long day of filming ahead.

Little did I know how long a day it would turn out to be.

When I got home after fourteen hours in the studio,

I went to my bathroom and took off my makeup. Then I checked my Instagram and saw that my post had exploded with streams of fiery comments. Unbeknownst to me, Bianca Del Rio (also known as Roy Haylock) had used this phrase on the reality competition show *RuPaul's Drag Race*. Bianca had taken it on as sort of her own catch-phrase, and it became the name and theme of her comedy tour. That evening, Del Rio regrammed my post on social media, with a derogatory, name-calling comment toward me. Soon LGBT advocates were flooding my page, objecting to my use of "Rio's phrase" and writing words of hate and anger on my post.

This exchange upset me deeply. First, because I knew my own heart in posting this picture, and no one likes to be misunderstood. My intentions came from a pure place. I needed a boost of encouragement that day, and I shared my post hoping it would offer the same to others. Second, the comments on my Instagram account were divisive and hurtful to others, and people were beyond disrespectful.

I want to live out my faith, even when the going gets tough. Maybe especially then. Because my purpose is to glorify God, I can look at even a difficult situation like this and see it as an opportunity to do what I was put on the planet to do. Barefaced in my bathroom, I stared at my iPhone screen and took a deep breath. It's easy to get heated up when someone attacks, especially for the wrong reasons. My knee-jerk reaction was to fight back, but I've learned that retaliation rarely results in positive dialogue, and my goal was to be heard, not get into a war.

I took a beat. I silently prayed. I thought about what I really wanted to say and responded to Del Rio in her comments section. Here's what I wrote: "Why do you have to be nasty to me? You don't know me or my heart. I'm not homophobic, and I'm always sad when people think otherwise. Loving Jesus doesn't mean I hate gay people or anyone. You sent a bunch of hateful people to my page writing horrible things. I hope next time you'll spread love and kindness, even when you disagree with people. Sending you love and wishing you all the best. Truly."

I'm usually pretty good at letting the negativity online roll off me. I usually don't engage with it, because you can't ever win. I don't want to spend hours of my time on a thread of back-and-forths, trying to explain or defend myself, because that person on the other side of a screen somewhere will never really know me and my heart if we don't have a personal relationship. I'd rather invest my time in the relationships I do have. The same goes for you when you're engaged in that Facebook conversation with a friend of a friend of a friend who doesn't actually know you. I don't think it's worth it. But every once in a while, I mindfully choose to respond when someone attacks my character.

One of the most difficult things for me personally is the divide between Christians and the LGBT community.

It breaks my heart when I see so-called Christians holding up malicious signs that say God hates homosexuals, and it breaks my heart equally when an LGBT member calls all Christians homophobic. Neither is true, and that's why I couldn't let Bianca Del Rio's comment go without responding to it.

I alone am not going to solve the problems between the church and the LGBT community, but my hope is to be a bridge builder. God calls us to love one another and to love our neighbors as ourselves. I believe this to mean Jesus calls us to love the people who are not like us, even and especially when it's uncomfortable.

And while Del Rio's post upset me personally, I am even more distressed to see the wide hurt and misunderstanding between these two communities God loves deeply.

For the next few weeks, this exchange was covered widely in the media. I had said my piece and chose not to engage in any further back-and-forth. Though I quit reading the thread, people continued to comment on my original post. Overwhelmingly, the comments were supportive, but there were still many nasty comments.

I believe the reason this got so much press was because even though I was attacked, I refused to be unkind. I didn't get pulled into a power play or a catfight. I just stood up for myself and stayed true to my beliefs. One of the mantras I repeat to myself in moments like this is "convictions of steel." You can push up against me or fire your weapons of criticism and disrespect, but I will not bend or break. God's Word is like a rod of steel that runs straight up my spine. The world sees this and is very confused. It's uncommon. But it keeps me grounded.

Media versus Reality

You see, these days, loud, emotional responses are the norm, or at least they are the responses that get the most attention on the news and through social media. Strong, negative feelings are more dramatic. The old journalism adage is still true: "If it bleeds, it reads." Even if what is gushing out of us is nasty comments and conflict blown way out of proportion. I guess that drives more website traffic than positive, encouraging, loving behavior.

We get used to seeing people handle things the wrong way. We see them blow up when a kind word could have defused things. We see them lash out and get defensive, and it starts to feel like everyone acts that way all the time. Or like you have to be brash, abrasive, and cutthroat to get ahead.

Lately I've been on the lookout for people behaving well. If you're like me, when you start looking for grace, you'll be surprised to see that the twenty-four-hour coverage of bad news doesn't always paint an accurate picture. Graciousness may never go viral, but the effects of small acts of kindness can nonetheless run deep.

The Truth + Grace

While on this mission to see graciousness from others, Val and I went to Best Buy. We'd just purchased a television, and we pulled up to the front of the store so they could carry it out and put it in the car. As we sat waiting, I watched as a man in his early twenties started to back out of a parking space. Two other young men walked behind that car just as he was slowly pulling out. One of them slapped the back of the car and yelled. The driver rolled down his window and said, "I'm sorry." But the man who hit the car yelled back, "Get off your phone when you drive, man." The driver repeated his apology. "Really, I apologize." I was getting nervous now, fearing this conflict might escalate into a physical fight. But the young driver kept his cool. He didn't get defensive. The other guy banged on the car again and said, "Get. Off. Your. Phone." I gripped Val's arm, hoping the TV would be delivered quickly. There hadn't been any real wrongdoing, but this guy was acting belligerently. We watched as the young man pulled back into the parking space and took off his seat belt.

At this point, I thought, "Oh no." The man who yelled got into his truck and slammed the door. The young man walked calmly over to the truck and waved, signaling to the other man to roll down his window. We were close enough that I could hear him. I held my breath. He said, "I just wanted you to know that I wasn't on my phone. I looked in my rearview mirror and, honestly, I should have looked in the side mirror too. That's my fault. So I apologize, and I hope you have good day. God bless."

The man in the truck nodded. He seemed shocked. When the driver walked by, I gave him a thumbs-up. Truly I wanted to hug him or maybe call his mom and tell her what a great job she'd done raising him! But I restrained myself. It was the best thing I'd seen in a while.

I hope this man's actions made an impact on the other man. I know they inspired me. Sometimes all it takes is one person's simple act of graciousness to turn our day—or maybe even our life—around.

Keeping Your Cool on the Hot Topics

Nobody really likes conflict. But it's critical not to let fear of conflict control us. God has been training me for years in this. In fact, He's recently given me *lots* of practice. At times, all that training drove me to tears and brought me to my knees.

I had the amazing privilege of being in millions of American homes every day on *The View*. Acting has always been my passion, and I've always loved the scripts and the story elements. So being on a panel talk show was not a job I ever sought out. As surprising and exciting as the initial offer to join *The View* was, I said no.

First of all, there were logistical considerations. The

show tapes live every weekday in New York, and we lived in Los Angeles. I didn't even have to discuss the possibility of asking my family to move across the country, knowing it was my daughter's senior year of high school, with my boys just two and four years behind her. I wasn't about to ask them to start over at this stage of their lives.

Still, it was a proud moment for me, knowing I'd been offered the job, even if I wasn't going to take it. But a new offer came back with some adjustments to try to make it work. Val and I had talked and prayed for several days through every detail it would take for me to consider saying yes, and the contract wasn't even close. So we decided to pass again.

Lo and behold, *another* offer came back with every detail laid out to address my every hesitation, such as flights to commute every week, working four of the five days a week so I could spend weekends at home, accommodations, and the ability to work around my previously contracted Hallmark movies and new show *Fuller House*. I got off the phone with my managers and stood in our kitchen staring at Val, stunned. They had gone out of their way to agree to our terms. I couldn't say no for any good reason!

As queasy as I felt about how our lives were about to change in this new season, we felt that this was a challenge God wanted me to take. We felt He was making a way. Motivated by my purpose, I saw this as an opportunity to live out my faith in front of a larger audience than I'd had the chance to connect with before. So I took the jump and said yes.

As thrilling as it was to be in this new role, I also felt a level of pressure I had never experienced before. I've spent my entire career memorizing scripts with storylines. I always had a sense of how the scene would end or where the plot would turn next. But here I was on live national television, and it was my job to speak into events and issues of the day, which are often controversial!

I knew God had given me this opportunity, yet I walked onto the set most days feeling ill-equipped to handle the challenges that came with the job. I felt *leagues* out of my comfort zone.

Although I'm very comfortable and confident sharing my opinion on social issues and talking about my Christian faith, I'm an amateur at talking about politics. I didn't grow up in a family that talked about politics or even voted. Certainly, I had formed strong opinions as an adult over certain issues near my heart, but I wasn't experienced in verbalizing them in conversation. I also didn't have the historical knowledge or background that many of my cohosts had when it came to discussing politics. And while the show producers told us they wanted to focus more on social issues than on politics that season, election year was right around the corner, making political dialogues inevitable.

I was the least likely character to be in such a position of influence. But when I thought about it, I realized there are so many examples from Scripture of what I call unlikely characters. People like:

- Moses, an adopted murderer who led God's people out of slavery
- David, a sinful shepherd boy who became Israel's most beloved king
- Esther, a beauty queen who petitioned a king to save God's people from annihilation
- James and John, simple fishermen Jesus called to be among His first disciples
- Paul, a persecutor of Christians, who wrote much of the New Testament after an encounter with Jesus changed everything

God has a long history of using unlikely candidates to bring Himself glory. One thing they all have in common is that they listened to and leaned into God. I did not start one morning without rolling out of bed and onto the floor. Sometimes on my knees, but mostly flat-faced to the ground, getting as low as possible to pray, listen, and put on the armor of God before heading out my door. That gave me a real sense of security, but it doesn't mean it wasn't tough.

Every evening we'd get emailed sixty to eighty topics

to cover, all global current events. The next morning, the producers and cohosts would gather for an hour to prepare by reviewing all the hot topics, adding additional ones that may have popped up overnight, and deciding which ones to discuss on the show that day.

We all needed to speak up about which topics resonated with us, whether we had a strong opinion about one or another, and whether we had wisdom or history on each one. I'll be honest: unless it was a social, entertainment, sex, or parenting topic, I'd get scared out of my mind. Because of my lack of confidence, I'd spend three to four hours every evening researching political topics so I felt somewhat prepared in the morning. It felt like cramming for a test each night and worrying that I might fail it no matter how hard I studied.

Sometimes I simply didn't know enough history or current context to understand the nuances of a topic that may emerge in open conversation. That alone was a lot of pressure.

Plus it was live television, so we had to be ready for anything! Walking out on the stage every morning was intense.

Some mornings, my adrenaline rushed even more than usual. I was a conservative voice, a Republican voice, and a Christian voice, and sometimes I felt pressure in knowing how to respond as such a representative. I could speak from experience but knew my viewpoint wasn't always going to be well received by those with values different than mine. And the media was the first to point that out!

It was tricky because I want to be a bridge builder, not a bridge burner, while also staying true to my beliefs. I'm not one who enjoys heated points and counterpoints, which is what *The View* is at times. I prefer to share my opinion, leave it there, and listen to the next person's, but I had to learn to jump back in for follow-up points to continue the conversation as much as time would allow. It gave me heartburn!

It was safe to predict that I'd be the minority opinion the majority of the time, because I was the most conservative voice at the table and outnumbered. I knew the others would ask me hard questions and challenge me, and that was to be expected. In those moments, my convictions of steel were a lifeline. But I can honestly say that I didn't take any of it personally. Opinions are just that: opinions. They are personal, but a person is always far more than their intellectual stances, and every person is always worthy of our respect, even if we don't agree with their views. Sometimes it's harder for people to discuss their opinions respectfully or calmly, because they are incredibly passionate about the issue, and I get that.

However, it didn't mean that I didn't have a million boo-hoo moments in my dressing room, crying and praying about how I would get through the show or about how disappointed I was in myself for not expressing my thoughts the way I intended to. I put more pressure on myself than any one person put on me. Just ask the show's producers; they knew when to steer clear of my dressing room or coddle me after a tough show, for which I'll always be thankful.

Dancing with the Stars also helped me learn how to handle conflict. We were under intense pressure physically and mentally. That led to relational and professional conflict that was often filmed for television. Looking back, I realize that my convictions of steel were forged in many furnaces, and God continues to stretch me and grow me. My prayer life is stronger than ever as a result of going through those seasons. The heat of the pressure just drove me farther into dependence on God. For that, I'm forever grateful.

Practical Ways to Handle Conflict with Grace

People sometimes ask me, "How do you not lose it when you're being attacked and criticized?" I got that question a lot when I was on *The View,* and I get it now whenever the media is dismissive of me in light of my faith or political views. Fans or viewers tell me they feel like fighting on my behalf, which I completely understand. What they really want to know is, How can I stay cool, calm, and collected when people are unkind to me?

Here's the truth. I don't always *feel* calm. Rather I'm mindful of my purpose—to glorify God in all I do. And that gives me an anchor. My deep desire is to extend to others just some of the grace constantly extended to me through Jesus Christ. My faith gives me presence of mind in those moments, and my prayer life gives me strength.

When you have a direct line to the Creator of the universe, you don't feel as intimidated by worldly things. I can talk to God about anything, and He answers. Not always the way I want Him to or in the timeline I hope for, but He always answers.

Having been in this business a long time, I've developed five secret tools that I use regularly to stay cool. You don't have to be an actress or have a job with intense public pressure to need these tools in your toolbox. We all face criticism and conflict, and we all need to know how to handle it with grace. Here are five methods I've learned along the way.

Take Deep Breaths

When conflict comes, I take slow, measured breaths—counting to three as I inhale, then counting to three as I exhale. Do this a few times, and it's like a mental reset. It's easy to want to rush to act, but a few breaths work wonders for the body and soul. Breathing helps me quiet the other voices so I can hear God speaking peace and assurance.

God's supernatural peace is promised to all believers.

Philippians 4:7 makes this comforting promise: "The peace of God, which transcends all understanding, will guard your hearts and your minds in Christ Jesus."

God's peace is available to me, and it will guard my heart and mind in a conflict. When my emotions start to surge, I need a breath or two to remind me of this truth. Sometimes a few breaths is all it takes.

Take a Beat

I borrowed this from my acting career. Taking a beat means sitting still for a moment to let the previous line or joke sink in. I often count quietly to myself. This does not always come easily. It's a discipline I've learned over time. But when I put it into practice, I always feel more in control, which makes everything much easier. I've found that when I take a beat, I can smile after a few breaths. I'm not talking about a pasted-on smile. I'm not ignoring the situation in front of me. But taking a breath and then taking a beat helps me tap into a peace that pervades the rocky moments. I've experienced that peace more times than I can count.

Switch Roles

After I breathe and take a beat to remember who (or whose!) I am, I mentally switch sides, trying to think about the other person's perspective. Most often when I do this, I discover that the other person's words or behavior reveals fear, pain, sadness, or discomfort. When I see the vulnerable person behind the fuss, compassion comes naturally. This is one way my belief that all people are made in the image of God plays out practically. We each have God-given value and God-given emotions. When I remember that my opponent in a conflict is an image bearer, empathy always bubbles up in my heart.

Go to God First

Sometimes I need to sit with my emotional response for a while. I need to name my feelings ("I'm feeling defensive" or "What they said about me hurt because I worked so hard"). I don't try to fight how I feel, because emotions aren't right or wrong; they are value neutral. It's how we behave that is right or wrong.

The Bible says, "Be angry, and do not sin" (Eph. 4:26 NKJV). In other words, feel what you're feeling, but don't hurt others with your words or actions. When we seek the best for everyone, a win-win is possible.

So sometimes I count to ten, say a quick prayer, and then act. Other times I may need to sleep on it before I can act.

But whatever the case, I pray.

God's Word says, "Be anxious for nothing, but in everything by prayer and supplication, with thanksgiving, let your requests be made known to God; and the peace of God, which surpasses all understanding, will guard your hearts and minds through Christ Jesus" (Phil. 4:6–7 NKJV).

What is the antidote to anxiety? Thankful prayer. That means I should be grateful for the person and the circumstance. After all, God allowed this moment into my life for a reason, whether for discipline or for blessing, or maybe so I could be a blessing to someone else. Honestly, I don't usually know why, but I believe that He is a good Father and that He has control. So I need to thank Him for all those things and trust. Prayer is how I do that best.

Ask for What You Want

Here's the hardest part of conflict for me: asking for what I want. It's my job to give voice to my needs and concerns. It's nobody else's job but mine. That's been a hard lesson for me. I could have saved myself a lot of heartache if I had learned it sooner!

Women especially seem to have a hard time with this one. Culturally, many of us have been trained *not* to speak up for what we want. But frankly, if we don't, who will? It's foolish—actually ridiculous—to complain about not having what you want if you don't speak up for yourself and ask. I'm not talking about *demanding* what we want or making requests in ways that are angry and entitled. But it has helped me tremendously to realize that I am the one who must give voice to what I need. Rather than simply venting my emotions or cataloging my complaint, I try to cut to the chase in a conflict and calmly, respectfully ask for what I want.

Here's an amazing truth I never thought I'd write. I've learned that sometimes I have to create conflict when my impulse is to keep my mouth closed for the sake of peace. It's my job to stand my ground sometimes. It's your job to stand your ground sometimes too. The challenge is to do it with elegance and conviction. To keep it classy by keeping it kind, no matter what conflict comes our way.

Your Turn

Wish you could have a do-over on a recent conflict? We can all think of situations in which we didn't handle things in a way that was classy or kind. Now imagine yourself back in that moment and picture yourself going through the five steps.

1. Take deep breaths.
2. Take a beat.
3. Switch roles.
4. Pray first.
5. Ask for what you want.

How might your situation have turned out differently?

The bad news is, we cannot go back. You cannot undo past actions, but you may still have an opportunity to respond with kindness and class. Could you make a phone call or write a note to the individual you are thinking of and let them know you wish you'd handled things differently? Think of the young man in the Best Buy parking lot. It took some guts to get out of his car to talk to the man he offended. There was no guaranteed outcome.

It certainly would have been more convenient for him to simply stay in his car and drive away. He took the high road instead. You can too. Admitting our mistakes is part of being gracious.

You also have the opportunity to do things differently in the future. Whether it's a tiny passive-aggressive comment or a full blowup, conflict is an inevitable part of life. We can't control that, but we can control our response. There will be plenty of opportunities for your convictions of steel to be forged and strengthened. Will you take them?

These are not easy choices, but we have good reason to make them. After all, it's your character on the line. But do you know what? Even when it's tempting for me to react in anger or frustration, I'm reminded that my character is precious and not worth wasting on a moment's flare-up.

Your integrity is worth so much more than proving a point or having the last word. Because when we lash back, we stoop to our challenger's level of meanness. And at the end of the day, that's not what we really want.

The choice is ours: we can react in the heat of our emotions, or we can respond with grace. As women responsible for our own actions, we can choose a reactive response or a redemptive response.

I vote we take the high road. Let's keep it classy and choose kindness.

CHAPTER 3

Kindness, Please!

Kindness recognizes the
image of God in all people

When I was filming *The View* in New York City, I rode the subway. Every day. Multiple times a day. Glamorous, I know! As a California girl, used to the wind in my hair, I found that traveling in the dark underground was hard to get used to. But any self-respecting New Yorker has a Metro card. It's just part of living in the city. One afternoon, headed home after my workout, I stepped onto the sweaty, standing-room-only subway car at rush hour.

Picture me wearing gym clothes, running shoes, a baseball cap, backpack on my back, earbuds in, trying to be incognito. Got the picture? Maybe this will help: imagine me peeking out from under some tall man's arm, trying to keep a grip on the germy pole while the car jerks and screeches to a stop.

As I stood there, a woman who looked at least eight months pregnant slid in and grabbed a pole near me. I stood there feeling helpless and anxious, scanning the car, hoping someone would give up their seat for her. I've been pregnant three times. It wasn't too hard to imagine how miserable it would be to stand in a crowded, jerky car with feet swollen after a long day!

But all eyes in the subway car were either closed or focused on phones. Each time we stopped and a seat opened, someone would slide into it before this woman could get there. It was so frustrating to watch. I could hear my mother's voice saying, "What kind of person lets a pregnant woman ride forty blocks standing?" Part of me wanted to yell at the other commuters, but I knew that wouldn't help. So I did what I could. I caught the woman's eye—a real no-no on the subway—and compassionately smiled. The relief in the smile she returned made my day.

Is a smile between strangers on the subway a little thing? Sure, but it's the little things that keep us going. The small gestures of compassion and kindness that give us strength to carry on in a crazy day in this crazy world. Maybe a smile doesn't seem like much, but in a city where people are so quick to get where they're going, where we pass each other by without any human interaction, it mattered to me. This woman and I saw each other, even if just for an instant.

That's the invitation kindness offers to you and me: will we stop for even a moment to truly see each other? Every person we pass every day, whether on the street or in the subway, in the checkout line or carpool line, possesses an incredible story, often mixed with beauty and pain.

I see you, sister. Some days, it can be as simple as that.

Good Reason to Respect All

When you think about it, we're all looking for a bit of simple kindness. We have a deep desire for empathy—some little sign that another person can imagine walking in our shoes. We want to feel valued, respected, and loved. And when we don't feel like we're being respected or loved, that's when we can get out of sorts.

We're all prone to feeling tired, overworked, and underappreciated. In those moments, we forget to be empathetic, to consider how the tired, overworked, and underappreciated people around us feel. Ironically, we tend to be least empathetic when others are unkind to us. Rather than stopping to consider what might be causing them to act so prickly, we respond by being rude in return. Rudeness compounds rudeness. It's a cycle that can go on indefinitely.

That's the bad news. Here's the good news. This is a cycle we can break, one interaction at a time.

Consider for a moment Genesis 1:27: "God created mankind in his own image, in the image of God he created them; male and female he created them."

Don't race past this. It's too important! What we read here is that humans were made in the image of God. Bible scholars call this idea the *imago Dei*. There's such dignity and holiness in this truth. God is the definition of all good things, and we are made in God's image! Each and every one of us mirrors our Creator in a unique way. That alone is reason for us to respect each other.

They'll Know Us by Our Kindness

I'm fascinated by the examples of Jesus extending kindness to others, sometimes in extravagant ways and sometimes in simple ways. When we start looking for these stories in God's Word, we find that they're abundant. I'm sure you can think of at least a few right now. Here are some of my favorites.

- He responded with kindness and compassion to the woman who touched the hem of His robe, hoping to be healed (Matt. 9:20–22).
- He treated the Samaritan woman with dignity, even though she was from a people group that others avoided (John 4:1–42).
- He extended courtesy and hope to the thieves who hung beside Him on the cross, even though they were criminals (Luke 23:39–43).

What strikes me as important is that Jesus' kindness wasn't conditional. Think about the chain reaction of rudeness we often fall into: If someone snaps at us, we're likely to snap back at someone else. If someone cuts you off on the road, you're apt to arrive at your destination frazzled and frustrated. But Jesus didn't base His kindness toward others on how others treated Him. He recognized the image of God in every person He encountered, and He extended kindness no matter what treatment He might receive in return.

What's more, Jesus did this for our example. He wanted His disciples to be kind too. Do you know what He said in John 13? "By this everyone will know that you are my disciples, if you love one another" (v. 35). That kind of dynamic—people being genuinely good to each other—is so rare these days and so, so needed.

It's probably safe to say that those of us in the entertainment industry aren't always known for our love for each other! I admit there's a great deal of ugliness in this business. Lots of beautiful people, for sure, but the pettiness and infighting could make the top reality shows blush! But here's the thing: I don't want that to be true of me. I truly want to honor what Jesus said, so people will recognize me as His disciple. And that means being kind. So what will that look like practically? I'm so glad you asked.

Manners Matter

When I was growing up, my parents taught us the value of good manners. I can remember my parents interrupting the family meal to correct the way I held my fork and knife, mandating that we write thank-you notes, and making sure we treated our elders respectfully. We were raised with the understanding that if a person didn't have good manners, they wouldn't get very far in life. Schools taught good manners too. We learned the value of taking turns. We stood in line quietly and patiently. We let older people go first. We always said please and thank you.

Today tolerance has replaced good manners as the ultimate value to be taught and practiced. There's a cultural mandate in America that we will tolerate any and all belief systems and modes of behavior. But have you ever thought about that word tolerate? It's a pretty low bar to clear. I can tolerate the sound of fingernails scraping the chalkboard, but it doesn't mean I like it or respect it.

Personally, I think we can do better than merely tolerate each other. What I'd like to advocate is good manners! It's a simple enough switch, but I believe that if we'd all use good manners, tolerance would be more peaceful and productive.

What do I mean by good manners? I'm talking about common courtesy. Good manners are the way we convey to others that we believe they are worthwhile, that they have inherent dignity because they are made in the image of God. Good manners are simply love in action. Isn't that more powerful than simply tolerating someone?

At the end of the day, do you want to be valued and respected, or do you want to be tolerated? I know which one I'd choose.

Here's where it gets interesting. Not only are courtesy and good manners respectful of others; they command respect in return. They will set you apart in a positive way and put others at ease. As you make an effort to be more courteous, you will notice that others begin to treat you with dignity because you extended respect, even in small acts like saying please and thank you.

The Science of Kindness

Still not convinced that manners make a difference? Does simply saying thank you feel futile in a culture where the clash of ideas and opinions has become so loud? Let's look at the science.

There's increasing scientific evidence that kindness is good for us! Which tells me human kindness was God's plan from the beginning.

Acts of courtesy and kindness have been shown to stimulate the production of serotonin, the chemical that calms us down and makes us feel happy. Kindness also produces endorphins, the chemicals that make us feel pleasure. And kindness produces oxytocin, which makes us feel calm, promotes social bonding, increases trust and generosity, and helps our bodies fight disease by strengthening our immune systems.[1]

....

1   *https://www.randomactsofkindness.org/the-science-of-kindness.*

Studies have found that kindness increases our mental, emotional, and physical energy while on the flip side working to combat negative forces like anxiety and high blood pressure.

Oh, and compassionate people—the ones who show kindness out of concern for others—have 23 percent less cortisol, the stress hormone.[2] Kindness is a natural stress reliever. How cool is that!

Not only does being kind have an effect on those around you; your kindness has the power to make *you* feel happy, contented, pleased, and calm. Researchers call this the "helper's high." It's such a rewarding experience that those who extend kindness to others are often motivated to repeat their actions in the future. When we realize that offering an encouraging word, an act of service, or a generous gift is such a pleasant experience, our brains take note and create a "positive feedback loop" that encourages us to act kindly at the next opportunity.[3]

What's so amazing about this is that the serotonin, endorphin, and oxytocin boost works for the person offering kindness, for the person receiving it, and for those witnessing it! Maybe this is why kindness is so contagious.

....

2 *https://www.dartmouth.edu/wellness/emotional/rakhealthfacts.pdf.*
3 Alex Dixon, "Kindness Makes You Happy . . . and Happiness Makes You Kind," *Greater Good Magazine* (September 6, 2011), *https://greater good.berkeley.edu/article/item/kindness_makes_you_happy_and _happiness_makes_you_kind.*

When others observe its many far-reaching benefits, they want in too.

Kindness sends out chemical shock waves! So if you're ever tempted to think your small acts of selflessness don't count for much, think again. Those random acts of kindness are more potent than you might realize, and they're likely to create a ripple effect God will use for good.

My friend and manager Jeffrey will often randomly text me, "Need anything?" I can't tell you how much those two words have instantly comforted me and relaxed me, even in the most stressful of moments. Just knowing someone is thinking of me and available to help if I need it is so reassuring. And every once in a while, I do need it. I've adopted this simple act of kindness from him; I like to ask some of my friends and family unexpectedly, "Need anything?"

Training = Habit

The foundation for good manners isn't just sticking to an antiquated set of expectations enforced by our grandparents. Instead it is this idea that we each have value and we ought to find ways to show it. Good manners are about putting others' needs first, before your own.

Val and I place a high value on teaching our kids to greet people well, to look them in the eye, to give a firm handshake. It's important to us that our kids know how to talk to adults. We remind them not to give one-word answers. When someone asks them a question like, "How are you?" the person is trying to engage. We tell our kids to be gracious about it and not take it for granted, as a way of showing the person that he or she matters. In our digital culture, the personal greeting has become somewhat of a lost art. These days, we can simply press a few buttons, and this is counted as personal engagement—liking a post, using texting shorthand, or sending a GIF to say happy birthday instead of taking the time to pick up a phone and call or send a card in the mail. These things aren't necessarily bad, but sometimes I think we take the easy way out when it comes to interpersonal communication, and I think we miss out when we do this. It's up to us to turn it around.

In a million little ways, we can use good manners to assign dignity to others. To train my boys along these lines, if I'm with them, I won't open a door for myself; they know they must open doors for me, as well as for other women. Although I am perfectly capable of carrying my grocery bags, my boys know they need to grab them, because I've taught them to be helpful to their mom—a lesson that will carry over to their future wives. My husband does all the cooking, so as a gesture of gratitude, I do the kitchen cleaning. I've also taught my kids that if someone leaves dishes in the sink, then as a courtesy to everyone who lives in the house, it's thoughtful to clean up after them, even if it's your annoying brother. Courtesy means you look around to see if someone needs anything. Through manners, we are teaching our children to put others' needs ahead of their own preferences. This means that even with two teenage boys in the house, loud belching is not allowed. Can I get an amen?

Should I Respond?

Certain sounds make me happy—my workout playlist, the sound of my children's laughter, the quiet rhythm of waves on the beach. At the same time, the world around us is often filled with sound that is simply noise. The Bible calls it "clamor." Out of sheer necessity, we sometimes tune out human voices.

Listening to someone and giving them your full attention may have once been society's norm, but today, with so many modern distractions, giving your full attention to someone is a *gift*.

I'll never forget the time I flew to New York to be on *Good Morning America* and was told that actress Kerry Washington from the megahit TV show *Scandal* was also there to be interviewed. Not only that, but apparently she wanted to say hi to me. I don't know if I can describe how much I was freaking out on the inside. I love Kerry Washington—like, love love love her—and she just asked to say hi to *me*? Yes, even celebrities get starstruck!

Although I had exchanged a few emails with Kerry, it was the first time I'd met her, and she made me feel as if I were the only person in the room. She looked me in the eyes and kept her focus on me rather than scanning the room for other, more important people to talk to. She asked me questions, like what was I there to promote on the morning show, and then told me how much she loved my book *Reshaping It All* and that she was proud of me for writing it.

"Huh? You read my book?" I was squealing to myself. Celebrity or not, when someone gives you their full attention, even if only for a few minutes, it makes you feel like you matter, like you're of value, like you're worth it.

In our modern culture of distractions, one of the greatest gifts we can give each other is to shut out the noise to engage a single person, one-on-one. We all have that choice to make in every interaction. Have you ever had someone listen to you in a way that felt really engaging? Whether it's two minutes or twenty, it always feels like a precious gift. Thinking of the moments when I've taken time to listen, I've found that often listening was a gift to me, the hearer, as well.

Sometimes kindness looks like generous listening. I've experienced my share of unkind words and actions over the years, when people chose to make snap judgments instead of listening. It comes with the territory of living in the public eye, I guess. I've developed a pretty thick skin over the years, but it still hurts when people make judgments and criticize me and correct me according to their limited insight into my day.

One of the hardest parts about being on *The View* was reading social media comments after a show aired. Producers tell you not to look at it or pay attention to it, but to me it was helpful to hear people's feedback, good or bad, so I could better understand how to approach a topic or articulate a viewpoint if the issue came up again.

But weeding through the junk to get to the constructive content would make just about anyone want to curl up and cry. People called me profane names and told me to shut up. "You are so stupid!" they wrote. Or, "#dumbblonde Candace needs a brain transplant." "You don't deserve to breathe my air. You are robot with your goody two-shoes. We'd all be better off if you were dead." I received comments such as these every day of the week.

But the worst comments, I felt, were the ones from so-called well-meaning Christians. I dare you to scroll through my Facebook page and take a look at the comments. It doesn't take long for the judgment of God's people to show up.

"You're a bigot and a false Christian," people tell me. In reference to a video of me dancing at a birthday party: "When I was saved, I was told that dancing in this manner was wrong and worldly. Just saying." In reference to a dress: "That neckline is way too low." Also, "She's a hypocrite-type Christian. She's one that looks back and gets turned into salt." "Obsessed much? So many posts are about her exercising." I responded to this one recently, deciding to speak from my heart and let people know that I'm a real person with real feelings, just like them. I wrote back to this woman, "It's so disheartening reading the comments. In my last fifteen posts, two of them were about fitness. The rest were about God, my family, and work. The people who complain only see what they want to see. It's not even worth my time writing this. To all of you who support me, thank you!"

I've learned, and continue to learn, to let most of it roll off my back. Certainly, I wish there were a button I could push that would illuminate in neon letters the words KINDNESS, PLEASE!

Here's why I use the time-tested maxim, "If you don't have anything nice to say, don't say anything at all." Can't you just hear your mother or grandmother saying that? Notice I didn't say, "Only say something if you can sound smart or wise" or "Only say something if you know it will help you win the debate." If it's not nice, don't say it! You'll be sparing the listener *and* yourself the embarrassment of saying something offensive or hurtful.

The apostle Paul gave this advice when writing to his protégé Timothy: "The Lord's servant must not be quarrelsome but must be kind to everyone" (2 Tim. 2:24).

Paul wrote these words more than two thousand years

before the World Wide Web, but they still apply. Perhaps online more than in any other sphere. There's a time for us to speak truth into the lives of the people we're closest to—our spouses, our children, our dearest friends. But if we've got something hard and critical to say, we must practice restraint. That kind of thing should only be said when and if you're in a true relationship with another person, when you've built trust and therefore earned the right to be heard. If I've learned anything about conflict over the years, it's this: hard truths are not for strangers. Some days I watch the news or look through my newsfeed, and the lies I see people believing are astounding to me. It feels personal. And I want to help people understand and see the hot issue of the day from a different point of view. But I've learned to conserve my energy. If you don't have a relationship with someone, don't expect to be able to speak into that person's life and be heard.

Respect No Matter What

I have a dear friend named Ron. He's a director whom I admire and adore hanging out with. I got to know Ron when he directed me in the Hallmark movie *A Christmas Detour* in 2015. He's always impeccably dressed, wearing a blazer, cuff links, and a bow tie every day to work while the rest of us are in sweats. He keeps a very fun and happy set, with music blasting between scenes and with his witty, dry, sarcastic sense of humor. He talks about himself in the third person and is unrestrained.

He's a gem, and I love him with all my heart. Ron is also quite the opposite of me in many regards. He's a far-left liberal, a gay man, and an atheist. When I started working on *The View*, I would post clips of my segments that were important to me on my personal Facebook page. Ron would post on his Facebook page about the same topic, but the antithesis of what I was saying, and it always seemed to happen soon after I posted. I usually don't engage online when my viewpoint is the complete opposite; I never engaged in Facebook debates, and I wasn't about to start. I also don't like reading into someone's posts and making them about me. It's easy to take things personally online or speculate that a barb is directed at you, when in reality it has nothing to do with you. But I saw his posts, seemingly a direct response to mine, three or four times in a row, and it made my heart race.

Am I blatantly offending him with my viewpoint?

Is he passive-aggressively responding to me?

Should I be taking this personally?

Is he wanting me to unfriend him?

It bothered me so much that I prayed about it for three days, and still I couldn't get it off my mind. My heart pounded every time I thought about it. I knew I needed to talk to Ron directly. I didn't believe dancing around the issue or brushing it off would be good for either of us.

It would build up fear and resentment in my heart, and what's more, I wanted to give him the benefit of the doubt.

So I picked up the phone and called him. He was surprised to hear from me but glad. I bumbled my way through an awkward confession that I was feeling sad and uncomfortable about our back-to-back postings and thought maybe there was something we needed to talk about. I told him, "You're my friend. I love you and respect you and your opinion regardless of whether I agree with it. But I'm wondering if you are sometimes responding to me with your posts, without having to say it to my face." I took a deep breath and waited to see what reaction would come. This would either be the end of a friendship or the beginning of a deeper one. I just didn't know which. And it wasn't up to me.

"First of all," Ron said after what seemed like an eternity, "the fact that you'd call me because you feel so bothered by this is mind-blowing to me. You are so bold!"

We talked about our posts, which he said really *were* coincidental in the timing. That's what we get for both keeping up on the news and current events! We even talked through our viewpoints on some of those specific topics, as well as why Jesus and the Bible were so important to me. We had a delightfully wonderful conversation, and I was so relieved. I knew this moment was going to build a stronger bridge for our friendship. At the end of our call, Ron said, "If there's such a thing as a good

Christian person, you just showed me. I appreciate that I meant enough to you for you to call me to resolve your feelings and not just sweep them under the rug."

It was connection, pure and simple. I didn't have all the answers. It wasn't about being wrong or right. I was simply being honest, courteous, and kind, and it made a big difference. I wasn't afraid to share biblical truth with him, but I wasn't forcing the issue either. We were just two friends being respectful and kind in conversation with each other.

Kindness Doesn't Mean We Always Agree

We don't have to only be friends with like-minded people. We simply need to be kind to all people regardless of whether we agree with them. We're all made in the image of God—no exceptions. And Jesus was kind to all—no exceptions. Who are we to think we can act differently?

In the end, that's what matters. Kindness, compassion, and empathy are values we can all get behind, regardless of whether we agree on every issue. Look, I know it can be overwhelming to see how the hot-button issues often bring out hate. Our convictions can get us riled up, and sometimes, as the heat rises, controversies can get out of control. It's easy to wonder, "How can anything I do make a difference, when the loudest voices always seem to win?"

I'm here to tell you there is something you can do.

Kindness isn't all meek and mild. Kindness is powerful, because—think about it—kindness transcends every barrier we can put up between us, whether religious, political, racial, or anything else that divides us. It's potent stuff!

Let's face it: we don't gain anything by yelling and scaring people. (When was the last time *your* opinion was changed through a heated Facebook debate?)

When there is conflict—and there will be—offer the olive branch instead. The easy thing to do is to react and condescend, to let our words keep pace with the hustle and bustle of our lives, to give back what we get. But we stand out when we resist the urge to be combative!

Some people hate being wrong. Me? I don't want to be wrong, but I see it as an opportunity to learn. I thrive on improving and getting better. I see failure as an opportunity to stretch and grow and to lean into my higher purpose—to bring God glory.

Your Turn

Maybe you want to be kind and have good manners, but in this upside-down world, you hardly know where to start. That's the beauty of manners. Little changes can make a big impact! Try these five things for the next month and notice the difference.

1. **SMILE, BE PLEASANT.** Smiling communicates that others matter, and your smile will infuse your own attitude. The more you shape your actions to respect others, the more you will believe they are worthy of your respect.

2. **OFFER A WARM GREETING.** Say hello and give a firm handshake or a warm hug. It's amazing how this sets a tone of respect and courtesy! To go the extra mile, as you greet someone, say their name. We all want to be seen and known. Speaking someone's name with a warm smile assures them that they are.

3. **PRACTICE GENEROUS LISTENING.** When someone is speaking, look them in the eye, not at your phone screen. If you don't have anything nice to say in re-

sponse, that's okay. Don't rush to fill the silence. When you have to choose between offering respect and offering just the right words, choose respectful silence.

4. **SAY PLEASE AND THANK YOU.** These magic words make a world of difference! My friend Ami noticed she was feeling grumpy each night as she was preparing dinner for her family. She realized she'd begun feeling a little taken for granted, so she told her kids there was a new rule: every child needed to thank her and kiss her cheek before clearing their plate, no matter what their reaction to the meal. The difference this made in everyone's attitude was tremendous! After a year of doing this, they now thank their hosts for meals when they're visiting with friends, and people ask her all the time how she has such well-behaved kids. Her answer? Habit! It's just a matter of consistently insisting they do the polite thing.

5. **PRACTICE PATIENCE.** In our fast-paced world of instant gratification and two-day shipping, we can get what we want pretty quickly. So much so that patience is becoming a lost art. People remark when they see it how rare it is. Patience is the height of classy! The next time you find you're going to have to wait, whether in the Starbucks line or at the DMV, think of it as an opportunity to be kind. Smile and be as courteous as

you possibly can. Those around you will be positively impacted.

Think of a time someone was kind to you recently, treating you with respect and their best manners. Get a picture of it in your mind. How did it make you feel? Why not try to recreate that effect in someone else's life today? You can start small and trust the ripple effect; remember those chemical shock waves!

CHAPTER 4

Dream Big, Pray Harder

Kindness gets ambitious

for the good of others

One night, my friend Shelene Bryan had a party at her house. At the time, she was a Hollywood film producer. But that night, among great food and lively conversation, something unexpected happened. A guest at the party saw two pictures of African children on her refrigerator and asked her about them. When Shelene explained that the pictures were of children she and her family sponsored, the guest scoffed, saying that the fifty dollars a month she and her husband, Brice, sent was probably paying for some schemer's Porsche. At first, Shelene felt defensive. What a cynical outlook! But then she started to wonder. Was the sponsorship legit? The questions continued to churn. She deeply wanted her contributions to this ministry to matter. She wanted to be part of whatever God was doing in these children's lives. She saw their faces every day in her kitchen and prayed for them, and she loved them from afar.

She had to know. So she did what only Shelene would do: she flew in, unannounced, to East Africa! She didn't have a high-tech plan. She didn't know the language. She didn't know the cultural customs. She wasn't even sure if she packed the right kind of shoes. She only knew that she couldn't *not* go. She simply showed up in a small rural village in Uganda with the photos and info she'd received in the mail, went to the local sponsorship agency, and asked to meet the children in photos GBB 8348 and GBA 8453.

A kind woman from the agency stepped up and agreed to take Shelene to meet the children. She led Shelene on foot two miles outside of town. Just as Shelene was starting to get nervous, her host showed her a mud hut smaller than her own walk-in closet at home. Tentatively Shelene pulled back the bedsheet that served as a door. And a smiling face beamed back at her—a face she recognized. It was the little girl whose photo Shelene looked at every day on her refrigerator door! Her name was Omega.

Omega greeted her with a huge hug and called Shelene by name. She'd recognized her from the family Christmas card the Bryans had sent—the very card imbedded in the wall of her hut.

Overcome with relief, Shelene realized this wasn't a scam. Her party guest had been wrong. That monthly allowance had been feeding and educating Omega. Soon Shelene was able to meet their second adopted child, Alonis, too.

Those few days in Uganda were surreal. Shelene returned to California forever changed. She'd discovered the daunting reality of poverty in the world and could never unsee it now. She decided then and there to start living differently. She says that comfort and security for her own family had been her primary purpose until then, but they were only part of the picture, and God wanted to show her more. In East Africa, she found true calling in helping feed, clothe, and house children in need. That's why she founded Skip1.org, an organization aimed at helping solve world hunger by offering people a simple challenge: could you skip something today—an expense, a little luxury—so that the money might go to someone with a greater need?

Talk about the contagious effect of kindness! Shelene wants to make the world a better place, she's using her talents to achieve that dream, and countless people have been inspired to join her through Skip1.

Each of us has been similarly gifted, with unique talents and gifts. When our gifts align with our purpose, we feel fired up too. We get the feeling Shelene felt—that we can't *not* do something. Those are stirrings, I believe, that are worth listening to. Those are the stirrings of the Spirit. That kind of drive—that fire—is passion. You might even call it ambition.

"She's . . . Ambitious!"

Have you ever heard *ambitious* used like it was a bad word? I have! It's the polite way of saying she's pushy and overly self-assertive and taking charge when she shouldn't be.

The implication is that ambitious women aren't virtuous or only care about themselves. I've heard this term used about women who choose to work rather than stay home full-time with their children, and in the workplace when a woman is climbing the corporate ladder, as if she doesn't deserve her success.

I'm going to call it now: that's nonsense! The women I admire most are ambitious. When they show up, they're fully present, sleeves rolled up, and ready to make things happen. Whether it's being a stay-at-home mom, cooking or painting, throwing a great party, teaching a class, or starting her own business, a woman who enjoys her work shines with a beautiful dignity.

I love what Scripture says about this: "Whatever you do, work at it with all your heart, as working for the Lord, not for human masters, since you know that you will receive an inheritance from the Lord as a reward. It is the Lord Christ you are serving" (Col. 3:23–24). I recognize my own ambition in this verse. Anyone who knows me knows that I throw myself 100 percent into everything I do, whether it's cleaning my home, playing a card game called Hand and Foot with my parents and kids, writing a new book, or searching online for the perfect dress to style a friend for her big day. I give it my all, my full attention and my very best.

When I say ambitious, most people think "cutthroat, competitive, ruthless." But I'm here to tell you that godly ambition, ambition that puts God and others above yourself, is at the heart of kindness. Using your gifts and dreams on behalf of others? You can't get more classy than that.

Dream Big, Pray Harder

I've always been a dreamer. You've heard of having a bucket list, right? Well, I have a big dreams list. Yes, an actual list! I thought about sharing a few that haven't come true yet, but it feels so personal that I want to keep my secrets between me and God for now, unless He decides to do something about them. Then I'll get to give Him all the glory by sharing with you! There certainly are things I've checked off my list over the years, and I'll continue to add things and check them off in real time. Checking things off inspires me to dream even bigger but pray even harder. Don't count me out for anything, because I just might show up in unexpected places! I believe our God is an ambitious God. His ambition is as holy as it is wild: to save the whole world! You can't get much more ambitious than that.

And because you and I are made in His image, I believe we are called into holy ambition as well. God can move mountains, and sometimes He calls us to join Him in this incredible work.

Maybe you're a dreamer too. Recently I talked to a young woman at the LA Conference for Women of Influence held at my church, at which I was a keynote speaker. Her dream was a career in the tech field. She wanted to use her gifts in the digital world for God and for good. But she had scoped out the industry and hadn't met a single Christian. She was worried that she might have to conform to excel. Would her drive for excellence mean she had to change her beliefs? Would being around people who didn't share her beliefs compromise her integrity?

It's reasonable to have some healthy fear about being the only believer in the room. I've been there—often! The music and entertainment industries can be especially daunting for Christians, because in LA or NYC, where I've spent so much of my career, our Christian faith is not always well received. And yes, you often will be faced with situations in which your integrity will be called upon. You will need to develop discernment, and it's wise to be asking those questions before you ever get in the game.

But being a Christian should not discount you from any dream God has given you. In fact, God may be calling you to be the only Christian in the room, so that others will get a chance to meet one for themselves and meet Jesus through you. You may be the only interaction with a Christian they'll get.

Call It Opportunity

God's Word calls us to be the light of the world (Matt. 5:14), not just the light of the church. This image reminds us to stand out, to push back against the darkness. Some people think they need to stay in the bubble, to only associate with other Christians and protect themselves from people who believe differently. I disagree. I'd like to encourage Christian women to be whatever you want to be and to do so with your ultimate purpose of glorifying God in mind. Wherever you go, just know God will be there too! He has put ambition in your heart for a reason. We need people of faith in every area of industry, to live and work with integrity while sharing about God's love.

I like to think of it in this simple formula: inspiration > aspiration. What (or Who!) inspires us to succeed is far more important than the goals themselves. *Who* you're working for—for God or for yourself—far outweighs the variety of work you pursue. My hopes and dreams for myself and my family are an outflow of my desire to shine the spotlight on Jesus' name. I hope yours will be too.

Who's changing the world? If not us, then who? Think about that for just a minute. If movies aren't being made by believers, they're being made by unbelievers. What about books, music, journalism, education? Who is leading the charge in each of those areas of influence? We need believers leading in tech, in science, in healthcare, in the classroom, and in the entertainment industry. God has equipped each of us for this moment, and the choices are wide open. Listen to the stirrings God has put in your heart. Pay attention to the things you can't *not* do.

Consider this: "We are God's handiwork, created in Christ Jesus to do good works, which God prepared in advance for us to do" (Eph. 2:10).

Our God is an ambitious God, and He has uniquely and specially prepared you to do the work He's calling you to. So go ahead, get a little ambitious. When you're leaning into God's purpose, it's a beautiful thing.

Claim Your God-Given Courage

Make no mistake: ambition requires bravery. You're going to experience moments of fear. But it seems "fear not" is one of God's favorite phrases. This power-packed little line shows up in the Bible more than eighty times. Be brave! Fear not!

So how can you be brave? Remember who goes before you and who is with you every step of the way. Don't you just love these words, found in Joshua 1:9: "Have I not commanded you? Be strong and courageous. Do not be frightened, and do not be dismayed, for the LORD your God is with you wherever you go" (ESV).

Joshua needed a high level of ambition to complete the task God had assigned to him. He was the leader in charge of helping God's people defeat their enemies and move into their new home in the promised land. Bravery and ambition were must-have qualities for this warrior-pioneer role. God spoke these words to Joshua as Joshua prepared to pursue all that God had for him. The reminders are worth repeating as we develop the ambition to pursue what God has for each of us.

Be strong!

Have courage!

Don't be frightened or dismayed!

God is with us wherever we go.

Every classroom.

Every audition.

Every conflict.

Every job interview.

Every opportunity.

We are free to pursue ambitions outside of our Christian bubble, because God is outside of the bubble too. He is present in the most unexpected places.

Is it possible to compromise when you're surrounded by people who don't share your faith? Of course. But staying inside the Christian bubble or ignoring your ambitions is not a solution. Do you think the devil stays clear of those places? That temptation only exists outside the bubble? No way!

Faith is like a muscle. It atrophies if you don't exercise it. Will you be in circumstances that test what you're made of? Of course! Will it change you? Absolutely.

Do you remember the story of Daniel from the Old Testament? I fell in love with this book of the Bible when I studied it with my women's small group several years ago.

His brand of belief—his commitment to the sovereignty of God—was completely strange in Babylon. And I resonate with this because sometimes my Christian faith is seen as wildly foreign and strange in Hollywood. So I perked up, knowing I had a lot to learn from this study.

Daniel was an Israelite—one of God's chosen people—and they'd been taken into captivity in Babylon. There, by God's design, young Daniel was brought into the service of the most influential person in the kingdom: King Nebuchadnezzar. In the king's palace, Daniel's behavior stood out. He prayed faithfully every day, and this was noticed in a nation where Israel's God was not worshiped. Daniel showed restraint and wisdom. The king noticed and gave Daniel some serious authority in the kingdom.

Now, because Daniel was getting all this positive royal attention, some Babylonian politicians wanted to dig up dirt on him to get him kicked out of power. When they couldn't find any dirt, they talked the king into prohibiting prayer. Violators of this new law would be thrown into a lions' den. There would be no second chances; this was a death sentence.

But when Daniel heard this, he stuck to his principles and continued to pray daily to God, simply because that's what he knew God wanted him to do. Sure enough, soon he was thrown in with those lions.

God intervened, sending an angel to protect Daniel. A miracle! When the king came back in the morning to check on Daniel, he was astonished to find him alive, the lions snoozing peacefully nearby.

Can you imagine the shock? That harrowing stint in the lions' den earned Daniel—and his God—even more respect from King Nebuchadnezzar. Daniel's integrity in a foreign land ended up gaining him a platform among the Babylonians, which allowed him to glorify God and become a prophet of their times.

The *Real* Danger

I hope by now you're starting to see that ambition doesn't have to be a dirty word. While I encourage women to be brave and ambitious, there is a danger there, and that danger may surprise you. The real danger happens when we succeed. That's right; I don't see danger in the risk of failure as much as I see it in the risk of success. Ironically, when we excel at something, the world likes to take that success and use it to define us. On the world's terms.

Because of my early success on *Full House*, the world wanted to define me as a child actress. Later they wanted to box me into my performances on *Dancing with the Stars* or my roles on the Hallmark Channel. Can I be honest? Sometimes I can get caught up in these expectations. There's a temptation to define myself by success, to think that what I *do* is who I *am*. That can be like strapping our hearts in for a scary roller coaster ride. Because when we have days or seasons when we don't feel successful or an opportunity falls through, we can start to doubt our value. When you define yourself by your successes, you'll soon also define yourself by your failures. A better way is to anchor yourself in how God sees you: you are His beloved daughter. No success *or* failure can shake this core truth of your identity.

I've learned that what I do is not who I am. Success or failure will not change the fact that I'm a child of God. I constantly offer my successes and failures back to Him. I simply ask, "What next, God?" and let *Him* answer. We can trust God. He is the one who planted these ambitions in your heart. He is the one who has a plan for you and lovingly walks with you along the way.

My Story of Ambition

I knew at an early age that I loved acting. I'm sure some of you or your daughters have home videos like mine, of when I was five years old, overly acting out the reading of "Goldilocks and the Three Bears." After booking my very first commercial for an insurance company, I was hooked. I loved the smell of the soundstage, and I loved the lights, the camera, and interacting with new people. I like taking direction and performing well. I like pretending to be someone else for a moment and using my imagination to step into their shoes.

Entertaining people has always brought me joy. God made each of us beautifully, uniquely, and with certain talents. Acting has been one of mine. Talent alone won't get you very far, though. I've had to cultivate this gift through practice and persistence, and I'm not finished yet. Natural ability may get you in the door, but it won't always get you the part. You have to try, try, and try again. Rejection is part of this process, and you can't let rejection define you.

There was a time I chose to persevere, when a TV show I was on for three years, *Make It or Break It*, ended. We were living in California and I was working consistently, but nothing had taken off in a big way. My husband felt it was time to move our family back to Florida, where we'd lived for nine years during his hockey career. I have always been very supportive and encouraging of Val's decisions for our family, but I just knew deep in my bones I was close to a career breakthrough. Something was brewing inside me, and I felt we needed to stay in Los Angeles.

After I prayed about it, I said to Val, "Please, let's give it one more year here. I feel like it's so close. And if after another year not much happens, I will joyfully move our family back to Florida, without so much as one complaint." I've never asked for something so big from my family. And it wasn't without internal pressure. I could tell he wasn't quite as enthusiastic about it as I was, but he agreed, knowing how important it was to me. He told me he never wanted to be a roadblock to my dreams. If Val had decided to move us to Florida immediately, I would have gone and done my best to respond to his decision with grace, but I'm so glad we waited. Because what came next? *Dancing with the Stars, The View, Fuller House.* Looking back, I feel like maybe that decision to ask Val to reconsider his decision was conviction from the Holy Spirit. My purpose was crystal clear to me. I dreamed big, prayed harder, and persevered when it would have been easy to give up. But God gave me what I needed to keep going.

I continually challenge myself to push past fears in pursuit of excellence, as I did on *Dancing with the Stars*. I've never worked harder in my life, dancing and rehearsing up to twelve hours a day and riding an emotional, physical, and spiritual roller coaster for thirteen weeks. Don't get me wrong; I'm not always able to persevere. The good news is, when I'm *not* able, God is able! He never gets tired, never quits, and never runs out of steam. He's so strong, even when I feel weak or discouraged.

Look to Your First Loves

So what's your ambition? What's your dream? Often the answer can be found in what you loved early in life. It's probably one of your passions, even if it's not in focus right now. Let me tell you what I mean.

I loved acting as a kid. It brought me joy and made me come alive. Then I put it on hold while our kids were growing up. During those ten years, I gradually started accepting invitations to be a keynote speaker at church events and women's conferences. Soon these speaking engagements began to fill my calendar. I enjoyed the work because I love engaging with an audience and love the opportunity to share my faith. But to be honest, it wasn't my passion. It didn't make me come alive the way studying a character and stepping into the story of a script did. My first love and passion has always been acting, but we were living in Florida, so it wasn't an option, so far away from LA studios. The speaking events kept me interacting with new people, kept me busy, were glorifying God, and were a good source of income.

But then I read this book, A *Million Little Ways* by Emily P. Freeman. The book talks about how those things you're doing that aren't your passion wind up hindering you from doing what you love. This spoke to me in a big way. After praying about it and weighing the costs, I decided to no longer accept speaking events indefinitely.

I decided to focus on my first love. I turned down every speaking engagement request for three months. At first it was really uncomfortable. I was unsure whether I was doing the right thing. But after my schedule cleared, my prayers and energy became so focused. I couldn't believe how much of a difference it made. It was like I had been released to do what I was made to do. I was free! Not long after that, I started acting again. And it was like that fire that had been smoldering was fanned into a flame.

If you don't love what you're doing, ask yourself, "What is my first love?" What makes you come alive? You might think, "But that's silly. I could never . . ." But why not!

Here's a question for you to consider. How might you edit your life to come back to your first love? What might you say no to so you can say yes to your true passion? There will be trade-offs, certainly. But there is great freedom in throwing your all into your passion and letting go of the rest.

If you ask me, life is too short. You can't go wrong with pursuing more of what makes you come alive.

Ambition Doesn't Have to Mean Career

Here's where I should clarify. Your ambition may not be your career. It might be using your gifts and talents in another way. Remember that verse from Colossians 3 that I mentioned earlier? It's worth repeating here. "Whatever you do, work heartily, as for the Lord and not for men, knowing that from the Lord you will receive the inheritance as your reward. You are serving the Lord Christ" (Col. 3:23–24 ESV).

Whatever you do, work hard to bring God glory. That means we work hard in our career, and we work hard at home, and we even work hard in our hobbies, because we're not working just to earn promotions or fill our bank accounts or win awards. We are working to fulfill our higher purpose of pointing others to the goodness of God. We are putting our ambition into action so that it might serve God by serving others.

It is possible to be an ambitious stay-at-home mom who looks for ways to better love and serve her children. It's possible to be an ambitious painter or sculptor or photographer who uses her gifts to bless others but never makes money doing so. Ambition isn't limited to career ambition.

What are you really good at? Maybe your first love is guitar. But then you realize, "Huh, I love teaching my friends." How about you teach guitar lessons? That's living in your gifts; that's being ambitious and brave! Maybe there's something you love, but you're not awesome at it. You love to paint, but you don't know any techniques; you love to garden, but you don't know what plants work best in your area. Being ambitious might mean making an effort to learn more about the things you love. It takes bravery to move a passion off the back burner and make it a priority.

Maybe you love soccer, and you need to coach. Maybe you used to write poetry, and you just need that outlet to bless yourself and the people who read it. Maybe you need to sign up to go on a mission trip or find ways to better serve others in their own neighborhoods. Make it your ambition to help. That is worthy, worthy ambition and drive!

I believe that God gave every one of us gifts and talents for a reason. If there's a tug and a pull and a desire He placed in us, we shouldn't have false guilt about pursuing it or ignore that drive to do more.

Have you seen the movie *Chariots of Fire?* If not, I highly recommend this classic film! It's based on the true story of two runners who competed for the gold in the 1924 Olympics. One of them, Eric Liddell, was a devout Scottish Christian. He was a runner and also felt called to the mission field.

In the film, his sister Jennie urges him to quit running, fearful that his Olympic training will distract him from his mission. She finally understands when he shares these words: "When I run, I feel God's pleasure. To give it up would be to hold Him in contempt. . . . To win is to honor Him."

In what areas of your life do you most feel God's pleasure? How can you honor Him by better running your race in that area?

How to Aim High and Stay Grounded

As I'm reaching for the stars, it's important to me that I stay grounded in my purpose and in my identity in Christ. What makes me stay grounded?

Family helps me stay grounded. My husband's perspective helps me stay focused. He loves me but reminds me that the entertainment industry can often push you into a self-serving mentality. That grounding keeps me sane! Val is constantly calling me back to ambition in service of others, and that's what keeps me grounded.

And my kids for sure keep me grounded. When I look at them, I remember that awards and good press and high ratings are small rewards compared with the incredible privilege of being in their lives.

Then there's my mom and dad, my sisters and brother. My best friend. The people I expect to be the most honest with me, as I would be with them.

All of these are people who keep me centered on ambition for the right reasons: to serve others, to practice kindness, to live out my purpose of glorifying God.

If you don't have this grounding with family, you have to find it elsewhere. Choose another family! Cultivate a trusted group of people who share your values and challenge you to be your finest. Be careful: these must be people who have your best interests at heart.

Maybe you're thinking, "How can I? I don't even have any friends." Well, that's where the church can step in. God's design is that the church would work like a family, since we are all adopted by Him. Join a small group. Attend a weekly Bible study. Find a team to serve on. Look to the church to find a group who can help you dream big while staying tethered to reality and truth. We need each other!

It may be a good idea to look to a counselor or someone who can give you trustworthy advice about your gifts and how to use them well. Whatever you do, *don't* turn to social media for these vital questions about gifts and ambition. Social media "friends" don't see the whole of your real-time life. Authentic relationships are cultivated offline, where we can drop the act and get gut-level honest with each other and support each other in the walk of life. We need real people who can look us in the eye and help us remember what matters most.

We need people who can encourage us to aim high, while lovingly holding us accountable and in check when our ambition leads us astray.

The Cost of Playing It Safe

Remember my friend Shelene? God reshaped her ambition in a mud hut in Africa. For a moment, let's imagine that her story had played out differently.

What if, on that night when a guest questioned her donations, she had simply remained defensive? What if she'd ignored the tug on her heart to double-check that her gifts were serving the intended receivers? What if she'd seen that impromptu trip to Africa as just another checked box on her bucket list instead of a wake-up call to do something more? What if she'd felt the desire to serve children and families in impoverished countries but looked at her own life and thought, "My plate is too full. I can't manage anything else!"

Tragedy, that's what.

Shelene would have missed an opportunity to live out her true purpose, and hundreds of children and families around the globe would have missed the opportunity to benefit from the amazing work Skip1 now does. When Shelene's gifts and passions intersected with opportunity, it was her ambition that connected the dots.

Make no mistake: ambition requires bravery *and* hard work. Shelene now manages a team with projects all over the world—and all the financial and logistical challenges that come with it. Being ambitious women means we are hardworking women, willing to go and serve and sacrifice to turn big dreams into reality. Holy ambition, to me, is the face of kindness at work.

Your Turn

You may not be called to feed children in Africa or to act in Hollywood. But you *are* called by God, and your invitation is now to discover what that unique calling is. Ask the Lord what His dreams are for you and pursue them ambitiously. If you need a nudge to dream big, consider yourself nudged. If you're looking for permission, the God of the universe gives it to you freely.

I'd love to see an army of kind, classy women infiltrating every corner of our society with their dreams to make the world a better place.

Getting started is often the scariest step, but don't let that stop you. Remember how I told you I love to journal? Let's journal together about our big dreams. Pull out your journal or grab a piece of paper and think through these questions.

- Define your dream(s).
- How does that dream relate to your greater purpose?
- What obstacles might hinder your achieving your dream? How will you persevere?
- How might the patience you're developing now help you in the long run?

My dreams and ambitions have fluctuated and evolved throughout my life, but I will never stop dreaming. Yep, I'm ambitious, and that's okay. God has used that drive, time and time again, to bless me and bless others. And He wants to use your drive for His good purpose. The world is waiting.

CHAPTER 5

Bad Hair Days and Bad Heart Days

Kindness practices

healthy self-care

Working in entertainment taught me early on to be conscientious about my appearance. Simply wearing my favorite outfit to auditions as a child—in my case overalls, Converse shoes, and pigtails— helped me feel comfortable and confident. That attitude helped me book acting jobs, even though I wasn't dressed in clothes as fancy or put together as those of some of the other girls who auditioned.

In the entertainment industry, looks will always matter, yet ultimately my desire to look and feel good is not about how others see me; it's about feeling my best. You may already know how much I enjoy working out, because I post about it all the time. But the reality is that the characters I play don't usually require me to have a lean, fit body. Being healthy and staying fit simply makes me feel strong and vigorous and more confident, which helps me grab hold of my day.

What's Even Worse Than a Bad Hair Day

Let's face it: sometimes our cranky, unkind behavior stems from feeling crummy. It's hard to be kind and pleasant when we feel bad about how we look or when our bodies don't have the fuel they need to function well. Sometimes a "bad hair day" is more about the inward state of our hearts than it is about what we see in the mirror. I've learned that the outward countenance and inward attitude are more connected than we might think.

I've made peace with the fact that I'm more pleasant when I feel good about myself. It's not just about my appearance. So much of how I feel is mental, not physical. I could be wearing the latest in fashion, with my hair and makeup done to perfection, but if I'm not working out or eating well, forget it! I won't feel as great or respond to others with the level of kindness and class I want to show. Feeling fit and strong absolutely affects how I feel. Honestly, I find that the days I have the most energy and feel refreshed and ready to bless others are the days I've made my personal health and fitness a priority. When I take care of myself, I find I pay more attention to the well-being of others as well. Of course, we all have bad hair days, and I'm willing to bet that for you and me alike, we're not at our kindest these days. The two are tightly connected.

The same goes for spending time in the Word of God. It's gonna be a "bad heart day" if I've neglected to spend time with God. God's Word is the fountain I run to in order to discover God's promises, to remember how He feels about me, and to remind myself again and again that

God is faithful. He can always be trusted. These aren't just lessons I need to learn once, or even every once in a while. Just as working out gives my body the fuel to function at its best, God's Word gives my heart and soul the fuel they need to live a fruitful, faith-filled life. God's Word changes everything. Feeling great inside and out involves staying in the Word.

Taking Care of What He's Given Me

Making nutrition and fitness a priority has the potential to become overly important, if it's an end in itself. If physical perfection is your goal, it can become an obsession. You might even go so far as to call it an idol. God's Word helps us see that an idol is anything we prioritize above our relationship with Christ. It's easy to fall into the trap of giving our time, money, and affections to something other than Jesus. But we don't have to choose one or the other, fitness *or* Jesus. Since giving glory to God is my purpose, staying healthy becomes about honoring Him.

In my first book, *Reshaping It All*, I shared my struggles with bulimia and my codependent relationship to food in my early twenties. It was a trying journey to recovery, one that I walked through with God hand in hand. Today it's that perspective and relationship that keeps eating well and fitness in perspective for me. Rather than it ruling me, I'm handing my life and my body back over to Him.

When you think about it, how can you have selfish pride over something that's truly not yours? Like the curator of a precious painting I didn't paint, I want to be a good steward of the body God created. God gave me this body as a gift. Would I be bringing Him glory if I dismissed or abused *His* gift?

Let's think of it a different way. Imagine I loaned you my car. Maybe yours was in the shop, so you borrowed mine while I was filming in Vancouver. What if I came to reclaim it and found that you'd left crumbs in the seat, left dirt on the floor, and smeared fingerprints all over the dash? Or the gas tank was on empty and the tires were flat? You'd never do that! Out of respect, you'd take good care of the car I loaned you. You'd steward the gift of my car well.

That's how it is with our bodies. God created our bodies and entrusted them to us. We owe Him the respect of taking good care of them, not out of vanity or conceit but because we are made in His image and hope to honor and revere Him. Think back to our earlier chapter about purpose. If your purpose in life is to be the most fit person you know, you'll find yourself constantly frustrated. Someone else will have been dealt a better genetic hand, have more hours to spend at the gym, or have more money to spend on a personal trainer. Fitness isn't our purpose; fitness is just one of many *processes* we may use to fulfill our ultimate purpose of glorifying God.

Hitting the gym isn't the only area where this truth applies. Rest is another area where I take steps to care for my body in order to better care for the gifts God has given me. Though I like to work hard and be on the go, I know that prolonged periods without rest make me irritable and vulnerable, prompting me to respond to the people around me in ways that aren't kind. Part of committing to being gracious women is caring for ourselves.

Consider the acronym HALT. I use it to remind myself not to respond when I am:

- Hungry
- Angry
- Lonely
- Tired

I have more examples than I'd care to share about how cranky I can get when I'm any of those things. The easiest examples are those with my husband. Nothing good ever comes from our conversations when I'm hungry, angry, lonely, or tired, so I've used this tool countless times to help me.

When I'm traveling for work, Val and I often communicate over a video app. It's just like leaving a voice message, but we leave a video message. I remember a time he left me a message that irritated me for no good reason and I sent what I *thought* was a neutral response, though apparently my irritation showed. When he messaged me back, it was his turn to be irritated, and the rest, well . . . you can imagine the argument that followed.

After cooling down, I rewatched my first message to him and heard how awful it sounded. I didn't see it or feel it at the time, but after seeing my scowled face get defensive and sharp, I realized how tired and hungry I was. The hunger and fatigue had made me irritated, and I totally took it out on him.

When I'm reaching to open the refrigerator or pantry late at night, I also remind myself to HALT, because I'm usually not actually hungry; I'm using food to try to relieve my loneliness when I'm on the road for long periods of time.

These external factors affect my body, making it difficult for me to respond well to people and circumstances. Yes, sometimes an endorphin-stimulating workout is just what I need to change my heart, but sometimes I just need to give myself permission to take a nap!

Your Works Are Wonderful

Reflect with me for a minute on what Scripture says about our bodies: "You created my inmost being; you knit me together in my mother's womb. I praise you because I am fearfully and wonderfully made; your works are *wonderful*, I know that full well" (Ps. 139:13–14, emphasis mine).

Did you see that? "Your works are wonderful." What

work is the psalmist talking about here? Not works of art that hang in some museum but the masterful work God did when He created *us*. We need to honor and respect the marvelous creations God entrusted to us. In addition to being faithful stewards, we need to be *gracious*. So many times I hear women downplay or even refuse compliments. "Your hair looks great" is met with a rejection such as, "Oh, it's a mess. I just can't get it to do anything."

I heard myself do the same thing when filming *Switched for Christmas*. My costar Mark told me how great I looked in my plum-colored dress, and I started to say, "Ugh, well, I don't feel very good in it. I'm bloated, I feel gross—" Then I stopped midsentence and said, "I'm sorry, my husband has told me it's unattractive to not take a compliment, so let me start over. Thank you!" He smiled and said sweetly that my husband was right and I should take the compliment because it was true.

We deflect compliments or try to undercut them by pointing out our faults. Friends, I agree with Val and Mark: I don't think this is a healthy habit. A simple thank you and a smile is the perfect response. Accepting a compliment is kind. Refusing one is like refusing a gift.

Taking Care of Yourself Inside and Out

We've all been through seasons in which we neglected to take care of ourselves, for one reason or another. That kind of neglect comes with its own consequences—physical, mental, and spiritual. True beauty comes from the heart, but I won't apologize for putting effort into feeling good and healthy and dressing stylishly. It is not about flaunting or showing off. It's about feeling good so that what's on the outside reflects what's on the inside. Feeling good about what we see in the mirror leads to confidence. Confidence helps us be bold, faithful, and kind. Because when we believe the beauty God has created in us, we begin to see it in others and call it out in others. We begin to see those around us with new eyes, recognizing the unique inner and outer beauty in each and every person. Again, my aim is to glorify God. I want to glow with the love of God, both inside and out!

These days, I spend a lot of time in the chair having my makeup and hair done for work. An hour and a half before the rest of the crew arrives to tape a show, Tara, my makeup artist, and Daniel, my hairstylist, are working on me to perfect DJ's look. As natural as it appears on camera, a lot of time and detail goes into making us look our best under the hot lights of the set.

The same is true when I'm filming movies or doing an on-camera interview for other TV shows. It's a time-consuming process, and it's not always fun to sit patiently that long every day. The good part is, I love the people I work with, so our conversations are fun, and it's two things less for me to worry about doing, since the pros are doing it for me. I use the time to multitask—learning my dialogue, answering emails, reading, and writing. I don't spend a lot of time on my makeup and hair when I'm off camera, though. I like to keep it simple and as natural as possible. That said, I am mindful that I need to take good care of myself, and I encourage other women to do the same, with the understanding that there are seasons when we prioritize other things.

A friend of mine read an essay called, "I Feel Bad about My Neck" by the hilarious Nora Ephron, in which Nora wrote about the increasing need for "maintenance" as women age. After my friend read the essay, she realized that while her kids were young, she'd been negligent in the maintenance department. She looked through photos of herself with those growing young children and realized that although she'd done a great job caring for them, she had neglected self-care.

She decided to take steps to change that. She treated herself to a new haircut and color. Then she went for a free makeover at Sephora's to get an update on how to apply her makeup—and get some free samples! She went through her clothes, which had begun to veer toward the "don't wear outside the house" category, and gave away ones that didn't fit. She started walking a mile a day. The difference astonished her. She looked and felt great!

"Friends and family noticed the difference in me right away," she told me. "That energized me to keep up the good work. But what really shocked me was how taking good care of myself affected my attitude. I felt calmer and more confident. Those things made me a better mother, wife, and friend. It's funny: Somehow I'd gradually talked myself into believing the lie that it's strictly what's inside that counts. Not taking care of my outside was damaging my inside!"

Seize the Day

Maybe you're not proud of your looks or the shape you're in today. Maybe you feel some shame for past decisions. Maybe you want to improve your appearance, but you don't have resources for nice clothes or makeup, or even the energy to get started. What steps can you take now?

Hold Up the Mirror of Gratitude

Let's start with a question: What's your best feature? Is it your hair? Your legs? Your smile? Your eyes? Your hands? We all have one! The first thing that popped into your head is probably the right answer. It's that feature your friends envied in school or compliment you for now. I urge you to hold on to that feature. Lift it up in gratitude and prayer! And honor it. It's your signature attribute and yours to take care of.

Maybe it's your smile. If so, make it a priority to maintain good dental health. My friend and makeup artist

Tara has amazing long, curly mermaid hair. When she was growing up, it was her trademark, but it was also hard for a young girl to manage all those curls, so she came to resent it. When, as an adult, she realized her hair was her best feature, she started to be grateful for it. She says, "On those days when I'm not feeling especially pretty, I'll wear a pretty clip in my hair. That reminds me that I have a special gift. And it lifts my spirits."

Speaking of Tara, one thing that is guaranteed to make it tough for us to be kind to other women is our tendency to compare. When you look at another woman and envy what she has—her hair, her body, her skin, her wardrobe— your natural tendency will be to want to distance yourself from her, to tear her down (even if it's just in your heart) in order to boost your confidence up a notch, or to want to discount rather than celebrate her God-given beauty. It's a trap! Gracious women know that constant comparing wastes precious energy and doesn't do a thing to help us look and feel like we want to. Tara's amazing curls don't detract from *my* appearance one bit. I'm bound to have a bad hair day and bad heart day if I believe the lie that says they do. Celebrating her beauty makes me feel better about my own, not worse. Kind and classy women celebrate the other women in every room rather than sizing them up. We champion and admire each other rather than resorting to undercutting or criticizing. God has created each of us with unique features in order to display His specialized care for us. Avoid the comparison trap. You'll be amazed at how beautiful celebrating others will make you feel.

I've learned that the best thing to do when I start to compare myself with another woman is just to acknowledge what I admire with a grateful heart, as when I see beauty in nature, like a sunset. I'll say, "Wow, you look beautiful!" It's fun to share a compliment aloud with the person, because it encourages them. I don't keep compliments quiet if I can help it! If I see someone looking good online or on film, I thank God for His good work in her. The power of the positive, grateful heart works wonders to displace envy.

Think about that thing that most troubles you about your appearance. Try being grateful for that too! At first it might seem forced, but truly, everything we have is a gift. Offering God thanks and petitioning Him if you need help works wonders. My best friend, Dilini, always talked about how much she hated the stretch marks on her thighs. After I had children, I too was bummed looking at the stretch marks on my tummy. Dilini and I tried all kinds of lotions and potions to get rid of our stretch marks, but they wouldn't budge. We decided to start thanking God daily for them. I thanked God for the three pregnancies that gave me those marks and for the good that my precious children had brought into my life. Dilini gave thanks because it meant her body had grown tall and strong. The thanksgiving started to pour out. After several weeks of deliberately talking to God about these marks that had previously made us feel shame, we had a whole different attitude about them. We now view them as our warrior scars! And when I think of one of my favorite female warriors, Wonder Woman comes to mind. I bet she wouldn't trade her battle scars for anything, because having them means she's still fighting! Our bodies aren't meant to be preserved like some exhibit in a museum; they are meant to be used! So what if we get a few scars and stretch marks along the way? Our bodies are gifts, meant to be used as tools to help us live out the lives God has for us.

God doesn't really need our prayers. We need them! Start lifting up the things you love and hate about your appearance, and you'll be surprised at how He works in you.

Before You Get Dressed

For me, clothes aren't just about feeling pretty. It's more about feeling comfortable, feeling balanced, and feeling confident. This can take a good bit of trial and error. Have fun with it!

Before we talk clothes, let's get one thing on the table. What we wear under our clothes makes a big difference. If you're wearing an ill-fitting bra, anything you wear over it is probably not going to look great, be it a fancy dress or a casual T-shirt and jeans. So invest in well-fitting bras and panties and let the saleswoman at the store help measure and fit you for them. There, I said it. I feel passionate about this. It's a small thing that can make a world of difference. No woman wants to feel uncomfortable in her underwear or be tugging at bra straps or feeling like her underclothes are too tight or too loose or too itchy. I say let's dress ourselves with dignity, starting with the basics.

Creating Your Wardrobe

What I wear should be the last thing people notice about me; they should see *me* first. I want them to see me as strong and comfortable in my own skin. And frankly, I don't want my appearance or clothing to distract. I want to be freed up to focus on being fully present.

I'm often dressed down for my workday because I will be fitted into wardrobe when filming starts. I don't need a bunch of clothes in my closet if I have key pieces I can rely on again and again.

My clothing choices are based on a few main things.

COMFORT. Comfort is key. Not necessarily sweatpants comfort but the sense that you're not distracted by anything—not the chill in the room (wear layers) or the zipper that keeps sliding down (a sign of shoddy construction). I'd rather have one well-made pair of jeans than ten that look good but feel iffy. It's just like when I was a kid auditioning in overalls; I love feeling comfortable and being myself in any context!

COLOR. I try to stick to a neutral pallet so I can wear

many pieces interchangeably. I like to have color around my face that complements my coloring. When I wear shades of blue, for example, I always get compliments on my eyes. You might consult a friend or do some Googling to figure out which colors pair best with your hair color, eye color, and complexion. Or aim for a few statement pieces—such as a bright cardigan or necklace—that can stand out among more muted classics.

MODESTY. I've said this before and I'll say it again: I avoid anything that's too revealing for me. I say "for me" because I know modesty varies from person to person, and it's all about what each person feels comfortable wearing. In my case, I try to highlight only one part of my body, like my shoulders or my legs. Then I have everything else covered. It makes me feel elegant but not exposed or uncomfortable.

SIGNATURE PIECE. It makes me feel extra special when I can wear one piece that makes me smile. Sometimes it's an accessory, like a piece of jewelry or a jacket, but for me it's usually shoes. They become the signature piece that pops. They are fun to play with, because of colors like fuchsia and mustard yellow and textures like velvet and glitter. Shoes give me the chance to experiment with boldness in style while keeping the rest of my outfit basic. A shoe style can change any outfit in an instant, taking it from day to evening.

Mom Knows Best

Since I started acting when I was five, I've been fortunate to be dressed by some of the best names and stylists in fashion. Honestly, I can talk skin care, makeup, and fashion all day long! But here's the funny thing: it turns out that all a woman needs to know about looking good I learned from being a mom.

I know it may sound counterintuitive. We have all heard the tired jokes about mom jeans and scarves worn to cover up spit-up stains. But in reality, a lot of being a parent is teaching our kiddos the basics. It's about uncomplicating the complicated. Now that my three kids are pretty much grown and are without a doubt the most beautiful children I've ever seen, here are a few lines I've preached to our kids and how I see them applying to me too!

"EAT YOUR VEGETABLES." You'd never expect your children to do well if you fed them junk and kept them sitting down all day. Kids need healthy food and plenty of exercise to thrive. Why would we think we are any different?

Beauty starts with how we feel. True beauty radiates from inside. For me (and for you too!), nutrition and exercise are critical to looking my best. I like to wash carrots, bell peppers, cucumbers, broccoli, and cauliflower as soon as I take them out of the bag, and cut them up so they are ready to go. It's in those rushed moments that we grab the worst snacks out of convenience, but a little effort goes a long way.

"WASH UP!" So many nights when my kids were growing up, they'd try to talk me out of taking their nightly shower. Did I balk then? No! So why would I let my own routines falter? I will not go to sleep without first cleansing my face. There's nothing like being freshly showered and clean to make me feel sexy and happy!

"BRUSH YOUR TEETH." As any momma knows, a smile makes all the difference in the world, and bad breath can ruin the best looks! So take care of your smile, and it will take care of you. If you drink coffee or tea, invest in whitening or use a whitening toothpaste. You'll be amazed at the difference!

"SORRY, NOPE. YOU'RE NOT WEARING THAT." Proud mommas make sure their kids' clothes are neat and tidy. Yet sometimes moms don't invest the same level of thought and preparation for themselves. Ask yourself these key questions.

1. **DO YOUR CLOTHES FIT?** A friend of mine recently lost weight through revised nutrition and exercise habits. Her clothes were loose and baggy. We're close, so I congratulated her and then gently shared that maybe it was time for some new clothes. She confessed that she was worried about buying new things, because what if

she slipped back into her old habits? I assured her that the opposite was the case: if she invested in herself, she would be more likely to continue her good habits. Once she saw it that way, she agreed!

2. **ARE YOU DRESSED FOR THE OCCASION?** Would we send our kids to the beach in dress clothes or to a wedding in a swimsuit? Of course not! Similarly, we need to consider the occasion before deciding what to wear. It might sound obvious, but who hasn't at times shown up in clothes that didn't suit the occasion? It feels awkward when I'm the only one in jeans when everyone else is in business clothes. When in doubt, err on the dressier side and aim a cut above. You'll never feel embarrassed being the best dressed in the room. Planning matters.

"STAND UP STRAIGHT." The first time I heard myself say this to one of our kids, I thought, "Wow, how did those old-timer words come out of my mouth?" But as a parent, I really started to notice the difference posture makes. A slouchy body communicates a slouchy attitude and spirit. My good friend Marilu Henner, who is my TV mom in the Aurora Teagarden series, took one look at my posture when I first met her and corrected it.

My whole life, I thought good posture was sticking your chest out, shoulders back, and butt out, like an eager child waiting for the teacher to call upon her. But that creates an S shape, which can weaken and strain your back. I failed to engage my core (pelvis and stomach) by tucking it under, so my posture was actually enhancing my lower belly baby pooch.

Marilu taught me to tuck in my tailbone, bringing my hips back in line with my body, and to pull my shoulders down, as opposed to back. A great tip is to walk as if your head were being lifted by an invisible thread that runs through the center of your body. It's so much more comfortable than the posture I knew previously. It's incredible what a difference this makes in helping us appear graceful and confident!

"SURE! BE A POWER RANGER!" When Maks was little, he only wanted to wear red. Red shoes, red shirts, red shorts. Red everything! It was his Power Ranger color. While I encouraged him to wear the colors that made him feel good, I have learned to dress like *myself* rather than trying to keep up with every trend. Just because something looks great on someone else doesn't mean we need to try to wear it. Put some thought into determining your signature style. What makes you feel your very best?

Maybe it's jeans and a T-shirt.

Maybe it's sundresses and sandals.

Maybe there is a certain cut of pants that makes you love your shape.

Or a certain fabric that makes you feel extra feminine.

Whatever it is, build a wardrobe that is made up of pieces that make you feel like *you*—confident and classy.

Your Turn

Yes, the bad hair days will still come. But I hope you'll invest in your appearance and style—*because you're worth it*—so your bad hair days will be fewer and your kind and stylish days will be innumerable! You're more likely to look good if you feel good, so take steps to exercise and eat healthy. Take steps back to the basics, develop a simple style, and work toward physical health. Rather than coveting or playing the comparison game, extend grace to yourself and others on bad hair days! And remember: the difference between a scowl and a smile is worth a million bucks.

Say goodbye to bad hair days and bad heart days alike by remembering that you are God's masterpiece, sharing a smile, and spreading contagious joy. That's the real secret of every class act.

CHAPTER 6

The Gift of Self-Control

Kindness takes responsibility

for its choices and actions

I n season 2 of *Fuller House,* we filmed one of my all-time favorite episodes, "New Kids in the House." Kimmy and Stephanie go to extremes to get DJ tickets to a New Kids on the Block concert for her fortieth birthday. Although the tickets they bought end up being counterfeit, unconventional events convince the guys to give them three front-row tickets. DJ's dream comes true when Joey McIntyre calls her onstage and sings "Please Don't Go, Girl" to her as a birthday present. Shortly after, Kimmy and Steph jump onstage, where they all dance with the guys to "The Right Stuff." Let's just say that it wasn't only DJ's dream come true! The truth is, Andrea Barber (Kimmy) and I truly have been huge New Kids fans since we were thirteen years old!

So recently Andrea, Dilini, some of our other girl-friends, and I went to see New Kids on the Block perform at the Hollywood Bowl. I've been to almost every NKOTB concert every year in LA when they tour, but this one was super special. Not just because we knew the guys a little better from having them on the show but simply because of the amazing group of women I was with. We sang, danced, laughed, and cried. All kinds of emotions welled up! This probably wouldn't have happened with a coed group, but with just us girls it was an emotional night.

We women tend to feel things deeply in a way that baffles men, don't we? We are in touch with our emotions. It's one of our superpowers! We tend to want everyone around us to feel good too. That's such a blessing, to each other and to the world! Being kind and classy flow out of that desire to make others feel good.

This amazing virtue has a flip side, though. Sometimes we let our feelings take control of a moment, a day, and even our whole lives. That's troublesome, because while our emotions are a gift, they shouldn't be sitting in the driver's seat. If we're ruled by our feelings, we start to make decisions not out of a sense of purpose or principles but from how we *feel* in the moment. We don't have the capacity to extend kindness to others, because we're too wrapped up in how we feel about ourselves.

Emotional decisions often result in regret. That warm fuzzy feeling of desire turns into a decision to cross lines sexually. The feeling of envy provokes a hurtful remark we can't take back. The feeling of fear leads to a decision to stay in a relationship or job that is toxic. The list goes on and on.

The Gift of Self-Control

I'll be perfectly candid here. If it weren't for my faith, I'd be an emotional wreck. I know my capacity for strong feelings, and I know that without Jesus I am just not able to keep those feelings in check. People give me props for holding it together when I'm attacked for my beliefs, for holding my tongue when others are arguing hatefully, for having a strong and loving marriage, and for having discipline in my eating and fitness habits, but believe me here: such praise makes me shake my head, because it's all Jesus, folks! On my own, I seriously lack self-control. I have tried to control myself, and without Jesus I can become obsessed with controlling other things. That's not self-control; it's fear!

The good news is that God is sovereign. That means that He has the ultimate control, so the pressure is off us. Do you remember in the introduction when I mentioned the fruit of the Spirit, found in Galatians 5:22–23? This is good stuff! We can't think of it too often. So here's a refresher: "The fruit of the Spirit is love, joy, peace, patience, kindness, goodness, faithfulness, gentleness, self-control; against such things there is no law" (ESV).

Did you catch that last one? Self-control. I can't drum up self-control on my own. It is an outflow of my faith.

My body, my mind, and my soul are submitted to God. What's more, He has fully equipped me to control myself. I guess it's not really self-control I'm after but God-control. I lean on Him when I can't depend on me. When my own emotions threaten to take over—whether it's happiness, sadness, irritation, anger, whatever—I just look to Him. Practically speaking, that means I stop and pray. I read my Bible. I pop in my earbuds and listen to solid biblical teaching and worship music. I hold on tightly to this verse: "God has not given us a spirit of fear, but of power, love, and *self-control*" (2 Tim. 1:7 ESV, emphasis mine).

Here's what that means to me. I don't have to achieve self-control. I already have it. God has given it to me! And it's such a powerful gift that it's listed with power and love! My job is to use it.

I cannot lose that gift either. God wants me to have it, and He will never ask for it back. I can fail to exercise it, but I have it for sure, because the Holy Spirit lives in me and will never leave me (John 14:15–19). Self-control is evidence of my relationship with God. Just as an apple is evidence of the kind of tree it clings to, self-control is evidence of God's work in my life. It is the *fruit* of my *faith*.

Don't Buy the Lie

What's important to remember is that feelings serve a purpose; they aren't an end in themselves. They come and go. The sadness, the fear, the anger—these will pass if we let them. Even positive feelings—love, affection, glee, joy, happiness, pleasure—are fleeting. Temporary. Feelings are not reliable indicators of reality. They're not even necessarily good guides as to how we should act or live. Yet so often we let feelings guide our life-changing decisions, decisions with consequences to our relationships, our finances, our careers, and most important, our character.

The truth is, our culture lies. Culture tells us that there is no truth, only how we feel about the truth. How many times in movies or on TV have you heard a well-meaning person say to the character in a crisis, "Trust your feelings and follow your heart"? Anytime I see this kind of dialogue in a script I'm being offered, I know I can't say these words with integrity. It's a slippery slope of logic that the Enemy—Satan—uses to try to trick us into turning from the truth of God's Word.

Trusting feelings to make decisions is like letting a toddler be in charge. If you let your two-year-old make the decisions for your family, you'll have M&Ms for breakfast, watch cartoons all day, skip naps, and spend each day in purposeless exhaustion! Toddlers don't have the judgment, character, even the hand-eye coordination for the task of running a family. You'd never hand your family over to your toddler, so don't hand your life over to your feelings. Your purpose and your principles are trustworthy.

So is God's Word. On the other hand, your feelings are bound to steer you wrong.

How do we make good decisions when our feelings threaten to overtake us? Let's look at three areas where we need God's help to use the gift of self-control: our bodies, our minds, and our souls.

1. Self-Control for Your Body

It's funny: we think of feelings as being something we can't see or touch, but feelings originate in the body. They're simply the outward evidence of something that is happening internally. Have you ever thought about that? Raising kids taught me that emotional outbursts from them (and from me) often happen when we are hungry, bored, or tired. Emotions were only the warning flare sent up to indicate a physical need. I learned to take steps to make sure my kids weren't taxed in these ways, and I applied the same method to myself.

I'm a nicer person when I eat healthy, exercise, and get enough rest. I find I have more energy to be kind to others and put others first. My body has a chemical makeup, after all, and those chemicals need to be in healthy alignment. It's funny, because I thought I was hormonal when I was pregnant in my twenties, but as I get older, my body's chemistry affects how I feel even more, for better and for worse. For instance, sugary treats can give me an instant superwoman high, but then when the sugar wears off, I feel awful, sluggish, headachy, and worse than before I ate it.

I've learned to make sure I don't get too hungry. When you're hungry or on a sugar low or high, you're bound to be testy. There's a reason the word hangry has become so popular! To help keep my blood sugar steady, I eat a healthy breakfast, like a protein shake, a veggie omelet, or a Bulletproof Coffee. I keep small healthy snacks on hand. (Assuming I will be able to grab something to eat on the go has gotten me into trouble, so I keep several protein bars in my purse. I've saved unprepared friends from getting hangry time and time again!) I eat regularly, listening to the cues my body gives me, and make sure to eat some protein and healthy fat every time. Avoiding sugar and processed food also helps me a ton.

Staying physically active is another way I practice the gift of self-control. When I start feeling overly emotional or begin to experience feelings of depression, I lean into the physical exertion of working out, whether it's aerobic or just conditioning. The sweat and the adrenaline work wonders for my attitude and give me a reset for the day. There are so many good psychological effects of exercise!

2. Self-Control for Your Mind

Self-control comes more easily when I stay in the Word of God. In fact, that's the only way I'm able to have it. When I fix my mind daily on what Scripture calls the kingdom of God instead of my personal kingdom, I'm fortified to live out my purpose and stick to my principles instead of letting my emotions determine my focus.

Let's not forget what Paul wrote in Philippians 4:8: "Fix your thoughts on what is true, and honorable, and right, and pure, and lovely, and admirable. Think about things that are excellent and worthy of praise" (NLT).

"Fix your thoughts" is just a fancy way of saying think about it. Paul's advice is that instead of letting our emotions consume our thoughts, we make the choice to think about something else. This becomes most practical for me in marriage during the times Val and I disagree. When I take the focus off what I believe to be his flaws and turn my thoughts to how I can better lift him up and help him thrive, things change. Knowing I'm honoring God by fixing my thoughts on how I can make changes in myself for the good of our relationship really helps me stay positive and let go of the negative.

3. Self-Control for Your Soul

Again, self-control is a fruit of the Spirit. It's a muscle I can develop and shape through regular use, but God gave me that muscle in the first place! The main ways I interact with God are worship and prayer.

Worship is feeling and expressing love for God, whether at church or in my car or in the kitchen or on the beach. Worship is what we were all made to do! When I sing about God, that's worship. When I lift my hands with excitement for something He's created, that's worship. When I live out my God-given purpose, that's worship too. Without feelings, how would we worship? I think that focusing our feelings on our relationship with God is the highest, most worthy use of them.

I love listening to and singing along with praise music as a way of worshiping. In fact, I created a custom playlist to listen to while walking through the streets of New York City and Central Park to work on *The View* every morning. Okay, a few of them aren't actual praise songs, but I think you'll see the theme here and how I turned them into worship songs to the Lord, knowing He has my back. Here are a few tracks that helped me prepare my heart for whatever the day might hold.

- "Soul on Fire"—Third Day
- "My Beloved"—Crowder
- "Able"—Needtobreathe
- "Priceless"—For King and Country
- "Devil's Been Talkin'"—Needtobreathe
- "My Shot"—*Hamilton* soundtrack
- "Unbreakable Smile"—Tori Kelly
- "Shake It Off"—Taylor Swift

I also talk to God. A lot! I'm so glad God is infinite, because if He were limited, He'd probably get exhausted by listening to me all the time! But Scripture says, "Pray without ceasing" (1 Thess. 5:17 ESV), so I know He never tires of it. As I've mentioned, I often write down my prayers. Prayers of praise, of concern, of request—no prayer of mine or yours is beneath His notice. The simple act of reminding myself of that helps me have peace.

Here's the Reality

Emotions feel B-I-G! But it turns out they aren't as important as we tend to think.

Isaiah 41:10 makes this bold promise. You might pick up the thread of a theme I mentioned in the last chapter; here we see those "fear not" encouragements again: "Fear not, for I am with you; be not dismayed, for I am your God; I will strengthen you, I will help you, I will uphold you with my righteous right hand" (Isa. 41:10 ESV).

There are a couple of powerful emotions mentioned in this verse: fear and dismay. We could swap them out for any number of strong emotions we might feel, and the truth wouldn't change. We don't have to be controlled by fear or dismay or shame or anxiety or sadness or loneliness, because God is with us. He promises to strengthen, help, and uphold us. His promises are stronger than any emotion that might swirl around in our hearts.

Emotions are going to threaten to overtake us at times. They are going to feel uncomfortable. Sometimes they're going to be so delightful that we want to grasp them and hold on to them forever. Since we can't, that's going to be painful too. But Jesus' promise is that He's got this. It's all going to be fine. There's no need to be afraid of feelings or to be controlled by them. Nothing can separate us from the saving, creative, nurturing love of God (Rom. 8:38–39). Not even our feelings.

With that being said, if you ever feel like you're in such a dark place and can't get out from under your feelings of depression or anxiety, don't be afraid to seek professional advice from your doctor in addition to prayer. While prayer is powerful, sometimes we can't just "pray away" intense feelings of sadness, depression, and anxiety. The way I see it, if you found out you had cancer, you would pray for healing, but you wouldn't stop there. You'd seek the best doctors to provide treatment in addition to praying. I believe it's the same for mental health. Also, don't ever be afraid to ask other people to pray for you and pray with you. We are stronger together.

Your Turn

So how can we practice kindness when feelings tend to overwhelm us?

Try using the body, mind, soul approach. When your emotions (good or bad) have you feeling stuck, ask yourself,

- **BODY.** "Have I taken care of my body? Am I hungry? Tired? Do I need some exercise?" Pay attention to your physical needs and work to meet them. You know how flight attendants instruct passengers, telling them that in the case of an emergency, they should put on their own oxygen mask before helping others? There's a lesson here for all of us. We are best equipped to take care of other people *after* we have taken good care of ourselves. When we tend to our bodies' needs, we have greater capacity to extend kindness to others.

- **MIND.** "Am I staying in the Word? Am I holding fast to things that I know are true, honorable, and lovely?" If this is difficult for you, save daily reminders in your phone of the truths you need to keep in front of you. Write the words of Philippians 4:8 on a sticky note and put it on your laptop or your mirror or your fridge, somewhere you'll see it. When a discouraging or frightening thought crosses your mind, give it to God.

- **SOUL.** "Am I spending time worshiping God?" It's always a good time for worship. Create your own playlist of songs to help you express your heart to Him and to encourage you when you're facing life's challenges. And don't forget to pray. Prayer doesn't have to be eloquent monologues to God. Prayer is conversation with God, and we all have our unique conversational styles. Perhaps it's time to find yours. Ask others to pray for you as well!

CHAPTER 7

Come On In

Kindness opens its door

and life to others

have two words for you, reader: carrot and cake. That yummy, aromatic stuff is one of my all-time favorites. I don't indulge in it too often, so when my forty-first birthday rolled around, I had my heart set on treating myself to a big slice of carrot cake with Val and the kids. That was the sum of my expectations for that day, just my favorite people and my favorite dessert.

What I wasn't prepared for was receiving a *whole* carrot cake made from scratch by my friend Leslie, and bunches and bunches (and bunches!) of flowers. My dining room table was covered with flower arrangements! It was the sweetest treat to be so loved on by family and friends. Seeing all those beautiful, delicate, colorful blooms and smelling their luscious scents made me feel cherished. That day made my face hurt from smiling so big!

When I visited my best friend, Dilini, at her new home in Phoenix, Arizona, she showed me to the guest room where I would be staying, and there on the bed sat a basket filled with bottled water, snack-sized packets of almonds and cashews, granola bars, a gourmet dark chocolate bar, a pack of gum, and a travel-sized toiletry set. What a caring gesture to welcome me as her guest. Because of her thoughtfulness, I felt like I was staying in the presidential suite at the finest hotel. I thought, "How great would it be if I could give flowers and special handcrafted gifts and baskets to my friends and family every day of the year?" Can you image all the smiles?

That's what hospitality looks like. It's thoughtful gestures that make people feel special and loved. It can be expressed in so many ways! Maybe through a heartfelt, handwritten note of thanks or a homemade gift or a gift purchased "just because." Maybe it's an act of service— like bringing someone a cup of coffee or taking a friend's toddler to the park so she can get a nap. Some of you are smiling at the very thought of that right now. That's the power of hospitality!

One of Life's Greatest Joys

I love having friends and family over to visit. In our super scheduled lives, having people over seems less popular these days. It never used to be this way, somehow. But with work, kids' sports, church activities, and music and school lessons, sometimes our calendars fill up and our lives feel like more than we can manage. Being busy has become something of a status symbol, as if a busy schedule is what proves that a person is valuable and important. Deep down, we know better.

Gathering together to eat, talk, laugh, and play is one of life's greatest joys. I love hitting the pause button to entertain guests. Together we put the demands of life on hold and just enjoy life for a while. I believe such gatherings are the kind of rest that our hearts and souls long for.

Because here's the thing: we need each other. God looked at solitary man in the garden of Eden and said, "It is not good for the man to be alone" (Gen. 2:18). That was the first and only "not good" God uttered as He created the world. Everything else in creation was good, but man being alone was not. It's good to get together, people. And enjoy it!

Besides, if you need one, there's a scriptural encouragement to entertain. Hebrews 13:2 says, "Don't neglect to show hospitality, for by doing this some have welcomed angels as guests without knowing it" (CSB). You never know who will show up for dinner! So treat all your guests with special kindness.

Our New House

We bought a house. It's the first home we've owned in LA in a very long time. When we saw the location, the yard, and the floor plan, we knew the house would work great for our family. We also knew that we wanted an older house Val could extensively remodel, and this one fit the bill.

So we dreamed together, Val worked his tail off being the general contractor for the project, and over the course of two years we've seen our dreams come to life. I'm happy to report that as I write these words, we're finished and . . . ta-da! We've moved in!

The house we'd been renting for the past six years was great, and we really enjoyed it, but having our own home—one we've imagined and created specifically for our family—is so special.

We've got an open floor plan—with big, wide doors and windows—that invites our guests to enjoy the view of the Pacific Ocean and the smell of the salty air while the breeze moves from the front of the house through to the back of the house and into the Santa Monica mountains. It's what I love most about living in California: the ocean and the mountains together in one view.

When we took the house down to the studs, I gathered the kids and Val in what would be the living room and prayed over the home. We wrote several Scriptures on the floorboards, signed all of our names, and recorded the date before they were covered in wood. We thanked God for the blessing of our house and offered it back up to Him. We pray He will bless and sanctify the time our family is here, but we know that it will always belong to Him and is our temporary home until we meet for eternity.

As we've settled in, I've been itching to host people in our new home. I can't tell you how much I'm looking forward to scratching that itch! We used to host a lot, but while filming *The View*, I was on the East Coast, in Manhattan, most of the week. The two and a half days I had back home with my family each week was too precious to me to extend to anyone else. We protected it fiercely, and we had to put hosting on hold for a while. But now that our home is ours to open, and I'm no longer traveling coast to coast week to week, we have so much to look forward to in gathering friends to join us in this space God has blessed us with.

Lifestyle Hospitality

Some of you are in that season now, during which for whatever reason you don't feel able to have people over. Maybe it's because you're facing challenges—health challenges, financial challenges, or a family crisis. Maybe you've just had a baby or you are caring for a sick relative in your home. Maybe you've recently moved and are still figuring out how to make your home in this new space, and you don't feel ready to welcome others into it just yet. Hear me in this: *that's perfectly normal.* There are seasons of life when we can't do everything we'd like to do, and that's okay. We have to learn our limits and respect them. Otherwise, hospitality will turn south very quickly, souring into resentment, and that's not good for anyone, host or guest.

The good news is, you don't have to invite people into your home to practice hospitality. You don't have to break out the fine china, put on a pot of coffee, or pull the guest linens out of the closet to extend a generous spirit of welcome to others. Hospitality isn't dependent on a physical home! Rather we can get creative and extend welcome in many other ways. Consider the other love languages that Gary Chapman talks about in his book *The Five Love Languages*. Then try showing hospitality in one of those ways.

WORDS OF AFFIRMATION. I like to express hospitality with handwritten notes on cards or stationary that I pick up in my travels. I know how good it feels to open up a sentimental card from someone just because. I love sending them to my sister who lives in Virginia and to my best friend, who lives in Phoenix. When I see a card or some stationary that reminds me of someone, I buy it and send it with sweet words to show the person how much they mean to me. I always love a good old-fashioned note via snail mail, which I think has become even more significant in our digital age. But I also love it when friends send me texts just to let me know they're praying for me or thinking of me. Some of my family members like phone calls best. Whatever the method, words are a great way to express hospitality. They're totally free! (Well, except for the cards and stationary.) And endlessly customizable.

QUALITY TIME. Maybe you don't feel comfortable

having people over, but you can still spend time with friends in other places. I like to consider shared interests and start there. Maybe you and your friend have been trying to exercise more, so you might ask her to meet you at the park for a walk. You'll both get a little exercise and fill your friendship cup! Or ask a new family at church to join yours for lunch at a restaurant after the worship service. You can also invite people to join you in activities you're already doing. Invite a neighbor to join you at your kid's sporting event. Reach out to a friend and ask her to join you at the farmers' market. You can even go grocery shopping together and grab a coffee afterward. You don't have to open your home every time you hostess. You can make people feel loved and at ease in lots of different spaces. Consider the regular rhythms of your life, then consider how you might open some of these spaces for someone else to join you.

GIFTS. One of my friends, Melissa Coulier, is an amazing gift wrapper. Anytime she gives me a gift, I never want to open it, because she puts so much thought and effort into the gorgeous wrapping, which has a special tie-in to the gift or something unique to the two of us. She uses stamps, freshly pressed flowers, string, ribbon, bows, and any other beautiful ornaments to make the box special. That in turn makes me feel so special. Spending lots of money on extravagant gifts isn't the goal of hospitality. It is simply to make others feel well cared for and important. Grab a ten-dollar bouquet of flowers at the grocery store, or spend a few bucks picking up someone's favorite coffee drink and delivering it. Gifts never have to be expensive to be expressive.

ACTS OF SERVICE. Another way to show hospitality is to serve others. How can you roll up your sleeves and meet the needs of others around you? My pregnant girlfriend Miranda posted on Facebook that she needed someone to paint her baby's room the next day since she couldn't do it herself and her husband was out of town. I looked at my schedule, realized I had my morning open, and texted her that I'd come over to help and would bring a few gal pals too if I could gather some.

Miranda later told me she cried over my message because she wasn't expecting anyone to help at such short notice, and knowing how busy my schedule has been made her realize how special she is to me. But that's what friends do, right? Thankfully for her, a professional painter also offered his services, and I'm sure the room will look better for it.

Oh! Here's another example. My daughter Natasha just brought me a cup of tea as I was writing this, which let me know she honors and cares for me. It really is that simple.

PHYSICAL TOUCH. A warm, firm handshake communicates welcome in a way that always amazes me. With eye contact, you quickly communicate respect. And while we're talking physical touch, never underestimate the power of a hug. It can make anyone's day brighter!

I just read an incredible news story about a police officer who pulled over a vet just to thank him. The driver reminded the officer of his own son, killed in action. The two exchanged a long, meaningful hug right there on the median. The gesture was simple, but the results were powerful in the lives of both men.[1] Shake hands, rub backs, give hugs, make eye contact. It doesn't cost a thing, and it can go a long way toward extending hospitality to others.

I'll keep being hospitable in all five love languages, but in addition I'm really excited about being able to host again. This house is a God-given gift, and I'm determined to use it to bless others.

Sunday Hosting

For us, Sundays are a great day for hosting. After all, it's a day of rest and relaxation, and that's what gathering is for, right? We have a family ritual in which we go to the farmers' market before church. We eat breakfast there and buy fresh food to whip up for dinner. Then we invite friends over for an early dinner at about four in the afternoon. We cook up a storm as a family, with Val as master chef (he's an amazing cook!) and the kids and me making the sides and salad and setting the table. Our friends start to

---

1 "Cop Pulls Over Soldier Who Looks Like His Dead Son, What Happens Next Will Shock You," CBN News (August 24, 2017), *www1.cbn .com/cbnnews/us/2017/august/cop-pulls-over-soldier-who-looks-like -his-dead-son-what-happens-next-will-shock-you.*

roll in, and the appetizers are ready to be eaten. Kids are playing, there's plenty of laughter, and sometimes singing! You can bet there's always a heated match going on over at the Ping-Pong table.

We love games too. I found these huge outdoor checkers that have kept us all occupied this summer. We're big on playing games for push-ups, meaning the loser has to do them. We're all about the old-school board games too—Monopoly, Clue, Yahtzee, Apples to Apples, dominoes. How about cards? We love playing Uno and Hand and Foot. Jigsaw puzzles are a personal favorite of mine and Lev's. I've been known to pull out a good one-thousand-piece puzzle and just get it started. Next thing you know, all the guests are into it.

For me, it's not about throwing a lavish party to make an impression; it's about people we love talking and laughing and enjoying each other. Conversation and a good time together is the goal.

When I was growing up, my parents often had friends over. Even today, you can usually find them playing card games with friends and family. When they hosted gatherings during my childhood, it was always clear to me that each guest was given respect and honor, simply because they were in our home. In a million little ways, my parents were communicating, "Everyone is welcome here"—young and old. (And nobody escapes from my dad's hilarious jokes.)

Another thing I could count on was that my mom's incredibly delicious secret recipe chocolate chip lace cookies would be on hand. At least until they got gobbled up. Yum! It's pretty hard to feel stressed and unloved when you're nibbling on a warm, homemade chocolate chip cookie.

Family traditions like these are a great opportunity to welcome others in.

When my friend Dilini recently got married, she invited every guest to join her in a meaningful tradition. During the Sri Lankan ceremonial portion, each guest who had helped to raise Dilini and her soon-to-be husband, Neal, or had in some way poured into their lives, was asked to come to the altar to receive a palm leaf as a symbol of their gratitude. Just about every guest went up, because every guest was that special to them. This reverent act stopped time for everyone and made us all feel special.

Whether it's a week-to-week tradition or a special occasion like a wedding, simple acts of hospitality can be that holy.

Crafting—and Keeping—
Memories of Time Together

Nothing makes us feel more connected in life than spending time together eating, talking, and laughing. Here's a tip. I always try to catch a moment when I just stand back and quietly watch my family and friends enjoying themselves and each other. Let that moment wash over you so you can store it up for the times when life gets stressful. Those moments are like precious treasures we can pause to look at again and again.

You might even keep a hospitality journal—a book to record the memories of your time together. Or, like we have, a guest book by the front door for our friends to sign so we remember our time together. Entries can be short and sweet, just enough to jog your memory: ice cream sandwiches on the patio with family and friends, game night with the grandparents, pizza party with the neighbors.

You might write down what was on the menu, who attended, any details that you cherished—twinkly lights on the porch, the smell of homemade brownies baking, or jokes you laughed at, stories you shared.

There will always be more items on our to-do list than we can get done, so take time to just enjoy each other. The way I see it, building memories together is never time wasted.

The Main Ingredients

If the word hospitality brings to your mind Martha Stewart's impeccable, type A personality preparations, I urge you to rethink. Remember that the goal of hospitality is simply to offer thoughtful gestures that make people feel special and loved. You know I love setting and achieving goals! When I keep the true goal of hospitality in mind, I enjoy hosting so much more. It's not about perfection. It's about finding practical ways to be kind, in your unique style. Hosting should be as pleasurable for you as it is for your guests. Get creative! Make it your own and you'll enjoy it! Here are my top tips for happy hosting.

FOOD. For me, entertaining isn't a fancy affair. I'd rather keep it simple. Homemade pizza, tacos, and salad are classics with me! My husband is such a great cook that I never worry about our guests enjoying the food. I only have one rule: there should be lots of it! If your guests feel like they're going to have to feed their hungry children at the drive-through as soon as the party ends, nobody will really settle in and relax! So it's essential to have plenty of food. Don't worry about trendy dishes and linens or perfect presentation. Just make sure everyone feels welcome to enjoy the food you have, even if it's just plenty of chips and guacamole or takeout if you don't cook!

MAKE GUESTS FEEL SPECIAL. Since we host at home, I like to tidy our house before our guests arrive. I imagine I'm a guest in our home, then look for ways I can enrich their experience of being with us. I might light scented candles in the entryway or put fresh soaps and clean hand towels in the guest bathroom. Maybe string up some lights in the back yard. Don't worry, you only have to do it once for the year! My goal is to honor my guests—to let them know they're special. Tidying up signals to myself and my family that the people coming into our home are important. I want them to feel comfortable and know I thoughtfully prepared for them. I don't get too fussy about it. For me, it's all about a tidy house, pleasant smells, a little ambient lighting, along with plenty of comfortable seating.

GREETINGS. No matter what size party we're throwing, Val and I always greet our guests by name. And if we don't already know the guest's name—like if they're the "plus one" of a friend of ours—we just introduce ourselves. That way, the guest replies with their own name and we just say it back to them. (Once I say someone's name a couple times, it usually sticks!) There's something really special about being called by name. It's a little way of honoring the inherent dignity we all possess. It's a little gesture that will mean a lot.

ACTIVITIES. I like to make sure there are things for our guests to do. Some people might love to just stand around talking, but not everyone is extroverted or even likes to talk! So I have puzzles out and games in various places for people to enjoy. If we see that someone isn't engaged, I might try to enlist their help in preparing or setting out the food. I want everyone who comes into our home to feel comfortable and special. There's something for everyone.

VENUE. You can host people in places other than your home too. When my best friend, Dilini, got married, we knew we wanted to throw her a wedding shower. Preparing for that party was so exciting! Just thinking about how special she is to me made it so much fun to think through the details—the venue, the guest list, the playlist, the flowers, the games, the gift bags. It was a joy to prepare, even though it was a lot of work. And we had a blast! The work leading up to it made the shower that much more enjoyable.

If you host in your own home, consider taking the party outdoors. Our parties spill out in all directions. Some of the best memories of gatherings we've had include front-yard games and backyard races, even while folks were congregating in the kitchen and the living room. When people feel welcome in every part of your home, they're likely to be comfortable and at ease. That's the goal!

That's another reason activities and games are great. They keep people moving and increase the chance for fun and for interaction between folks you might not have expected, like the toddler playing horseshoes with the teenagers. These are the moments I treasure in my heart. It's poetry in motion, I tell you!

GUEST LIST. At our house, we love to invite kids *and* adults to our home. We want all ages to feel equally welcome. If you've only thrown parties for adults, or for kids, you're in for a treat! Again, having games gives everyone a common purpose and bridges the gap between the kids and the adults. Sometimes we'll invite someone new, and when they walk in, I can see the look on an adult's face— like, "Wait, kids were invited?" But then we get them playing along, and they end up having a blast. I love it when that happens!

One caution: I avoid inviting so many people that the space becomes crowded. While I enjoy a bustling house, I've learned that when we have too many people over, I can't spend individual time with each person. When that happens, I run the risk of making people feel unwelcome, and that's the opposite of what I want! Unless it's a party, we keep our dinner guests to about six adults maximum and however many kids they have.

CONVERSATION. Sometimes hosts feel obliged to talk, but as hostess, the best way to honor my guests is to listen and to get people talking to each other. I try to speak to each guest personally for at least a few moments. I'll ask them about something that will make them proud or happy—something to make them smile. When possible, I'll steer them into conversation with others. Some people are reluctant to talk. If that's the case, I enlist their help. Everyone likes to feel needed and helpful, so ask for help in the kitchen or with the games. Sometimes I'll even assign another guest to make others feel welcome. The more your guests feel at home, the happier they'll be.

Your Turn

Let's be honest. We've all had some failed attempts at hosting in the past. Maybe you've decided because of that lumpy fettuccini alfredo dinner party that you'll never host again. Been there! Or maybe you've been in a hosting hiatus, but you're feeling energized to celebrate again.

Here's the good news. There's no perfect party. When you don't take it too seriously (avoid Pinterest!) and just think of hosting as a fun way to connect with people, you'll be freed up to enjoy it.

I challenge you to start now. Think of two or three people you'd like to have over, and text or call them today!

CHAPTER 8

Graciously Bold

Kindness steps forward in
confidence for what's right

Filming in front of a live studio audience requires confidence. It's not for the faint of heart. You'd think I'd be used to it, since I've been in front of a camera since before I was in my double digits. But even today my heart races with adrenaline and excitement, like I've had five cups of coffee. And it's not just the actors who need confidence. It takes a lot of hardworking professionals just to get those cameras rolling. Our crew for *Fuller House* consists of about 170 people!

That's just one of countless reasons I'm grateful to work with the team on *Fuller House*. Andrea Barber, Jodie Sweetin, and I grew up acting together on *Full House*. Who knew that when they cast us three unknown young girls, we'd end up having this incredible chemistry, connection, and love for one another, as pure and genuine as that of any real-life sisters. I believe it's part of what makes both *Full House* and *Fuller House* so beloved by millions of people around the world; you can see and feel that our love for one another—every character on the show—is honest, true, and real.

To have this happen is a rarity on a television show.

There must have been a little bit of fairy dust in the air when they put us all together that day, because it's been magical. We have a thirty-year history together, on-screen and off-screen, that goes back to fighting over sharing a bedroom, having our first on-screen kisses with equally awkward teen boys, getting our driver's licenses, and graduating high school and college, all the way up to marriage as well as supporting each other through divorce, our careers, having children, and all living together again under the same TV roof. I've done life with these two women almost as long and as closely as I have with my real-life sisters Bridgette and Melissa. To say I'm blessed getting to work with them again and see them almost every day would be an understatement. We really are the SheWolf Pack!

During the filming of season 1, for a sold-out live audience, we kind of held our breath. The results were way beyond what we'd expected. The audience went crazy! People were overwhelmed—crying, screaming, and cheering simply at the sight of the living room and kitchen sets when the curtains went up at the start of the show. Every time one of our characters made their first entrance, the audience screamed and cheered wildly and unapologetically. And yes, the loudest and longest screams are still for Uncle J, aka John Stamos. This thrilled us, of course, and the nostalgic relief was what fans had been waiting for. We crossed our fingers and prayed that the mass audience watching on Netflix would feel the same way.

When *Fuller House* aired on Netflix, the response was beyond incredible. The Teen Choice Awards fans voted *Fuller House* their favorite TV comedy and voted me their favorite TV actress in a TV comedy two years in a row. *Fuller House* also won the Kids' Choice Award and the People's Choice Award for favorite TV comedy in 2017. I believe we are the first show in history to sweep all three Choice awards shows across the generational demographics in the same year. We were thrilled! Advanced Symphony Media called *Fuller House* the most watched TV show of 2016, topping cult favorites like *The Walking Dead* and *Empire*. Something we were doing was clearly working, and new and old fans, some of them waiting as long as thirty years, tuned in to watch.

Behind the Scenes

It had taken years for Jeff Franklin, our creator and executive producer, to put all the pieces in place to reprise *Full House* with *Fuller House*. That made the fan feedback even sweeter. Many loved it for the nostalgia factor. The first few notes of the theme song alone had people dancing and singing. Other fans were happy we'd brought back characters they've loved since childhood. Parents got to introduce their kids to old friends and watch together.

But perhaps most of all, people responded to the fact that we were making a fun, contemporary, family-friendly show in which the genuine characters learn from each other, grow together, and love one another unconditionally. It's the kind of show that not only entertains you with silly laughs and a few tears but makes you feel like you're a part of our family too. Creating current content but staying true to the heart of the original *Full House* meant we aligned with our original fans and made a whole bunch of new ones. So it looked to us like that first season was a risk that paid off. And truly it was such a rush to be together again, to be part of something bigger than ourselves. Netflix quickly gave us the go-ahead for season 2, and we quickly settled back into our eight- to twelve-hour days on set, filming another round of thirteen episodes.

But then there was a change in the program.

Should I Speak Up?

Two weeks into filming season 2, I was at home with Val and the kids after a full day's work when the next week's script popped up in my inbox. Excited to find out what was going to happen in the next episode, I dove right in.

After reading it, I stepped outside into my back yard for some fresh air. My mind was racing and my heart was pounding. There were too many lines of dialogue, jokes, and plot points in it that felt completely wrong to me.

I thought, "Did we just get a whole new batch of writers in the last three hours? Because the tone of this script doesn't feel like the show we've been working on." I wondered how the storyline for the kids had been written and approved by so many executives when, as a mom, it was obvious that the themes were more mature in content, and I felt they were pushing the kids' characters ahead into situations that did not feel age-appropriate.

Not only did I feel that this script was unrepresentative of our show's brand; I felt a personal responsibility to make things right for the families with children who would watch it. I felt that I needed to speak up. But I also knew full well that to ask the show's executives to scrap and rewrite an entire script just days before filming would be considered nuts! What was I to do?

While I'm a confident person and not afraid of confrontation, I don't enjoy conflict. So to be honest, I'd have preferred to not rock the boat. But there was no denying that something in me was saying, "Candace, you can't stay silent on this." So I talked to Val and talked to my mom, who always has good insight, and prayed (and prayed some more). That prompting inside to speak up remained, with a fluttering of my heart—always my telltale sign that I'd better pay attention to whatever it is God has put there.

That was it for me. I knew I had to talk with the executive producers. As uncomfortable as it might be, speaking up for myself and the fans was necessary. I'd need to take this as an opportunity to assert myself as a businesswoman, a concerned parent, and a representative for the family brand of our show that I'd been part of for the better part of three decades.

So I did something that summoned my courage: I called and asked to meet with two of the executive producers the next morning to discuss the script.

To be clear, I'm not an executive or producer on *Fuller House*, just an actor. The producers don't have to listen to anything we actors say if they don't want to. But out of mutual respect for our positions and the insight we bring to our characters, they willingly listen to our notes and suggestions and make adjustments according to what they think is best. In fact, we talk through our notes at the end of each rehearsal day, collaborating to bring out the best in each scene.

But that being said, I have little control over the final say. I can tell them I don't like a specific joke or that something isn't working, but if they don't agree and want to keep it, they can and will. They have the final say. And there's not much more I can do about it.

Thankfully, it doesn't happen too often, though I knew this particular script needed more than a few line changes. It needed a major overhaul, and I was going to be the one to tell the producers.

Preparation Paves the Way for Confidence

Once I knew the meeting was a go, I prayed. A lot! I took time to outline my thoughts and verbalize them to myself so I could effectively communicate my position. For me, knowing what I'm going to say is a key part of preparing. As an actress, this is important to me. This was too important for me to wing it or speak solely from emotions. I was making a bold request, and I wanted to craft it carefully to ensure my best chances for a positive response.

Then I gave a good deal of thought to the producers' position, respecting where they were coming from. I tried to imagine what it'd be like to be in their shoes. I like what author Stephen R. Covey says: "Seek first to understand, then to be understood." The more we're able to read people, the more we're able to connect with them. I thought about these two men I'd known for thirty-plus years. When the relationship began, I was a nine-year-old child. I realized that they probably thought, "We knew Candace when she wore overalls!" It was certainly different for all of us now, me sitting with them at forty years old, about to have a very passionate and serious discussion as a businesswoman in my own right.

I thought about how they might perceive me in our meeting. Would they see me as difficult and arrogant? I wanted to make sure that didn't happen. I never want to be that person. After all, standing your ground is not arrogance; *it's faithfulness.* Being faithful doesn't demand defensiveness or abruptness; simple conviction is enough. It's not about being abrasive; it's about being graciously bold. I wanted them to know I was serious and not shy about my convictions. My goal was to simply and respectfully tell them how I felt.

So we sat down together, and suddenly it was go-time. I shared my concerns with the script, describing what I'd been hearing from viewers, as well as my own personal convictions, and how the script didn't jibe well with either. I reminded them that the reason viewers were connecting with this show was because it sought wholesome values, heart, and lessons learned. When the characters get into a predicament or make a bad decision, it gets discussed with wisdom from a loved one and with compassion and care and appropriate consequences if necessary. Even though we are a form of entertainment and these characters are fictitious, millions of people look to our show as an example for family. And I believe stories, by way of example, can show us a better way to live.

I didn't want our family brand to be compromised, I said, and I certainly didn't want our audience to lose their resonance with the show we had recreated. I was firm but friendly. I took deep breaths and spoke slowly and calmly. And they listened respectfully, giving me their full attention.

After they heard me out, they said, "Candace, thank you for sharing your concerns. After hearing your thoughts, we do agree that we may have missed the mark on some of this script's direction. Not all of us are parents, so we value your input greatly in this area. But also, some of the things you mentioned just aren't realistic. Not everyone has the same worldview as you, and while we know that some of our audience shares that, we need to represent all different perspectives. But we certainly don't want to compromise what our show stands for, so we appreciate the conversation and will take all of this into consideration."

I completely understood and agreed. I was grateful that these two men I've admired as my bosses for so many years had taken the time to have an open dialogue with me and were honest. It was all I could ask for.

The Only Thing You Can Truly Control? Your Own Behavior

That conversation wasn't easy, but you know what? I had confidence because I did what I thought was right. I did it strongly and kindly. I had prepped and worked hard not to be emotional or flustered at this meeting. I wanted the producers to take me seriously, which meant I was committed to speaking objectively and thoughtfully. I'm happy to report that after our meeting, they decided to retool the entire show, working out a more age-appropriate storyline for the kids, along with more appropriate parental responses. There were still some lines I would have liked to see disappear, but overall it was a huge win for courage, conviction, and family programming. And I'm so grateful our producers were willing to hear me out, honestly weigh my concerns, and change course as a result, which I know wasn't an easy task on such a short timeline.

The way I see it, I'm not called to rid the world of everything offensive. I am responsible only for my personal actions. My job is to live out my purpose: to glorify God in everything I do. If I'm doing that, if I'm taking responsibility for my personal integrity and doing my part, then I'm making a difference, despite the wins and losses. If I don't get 100 percent of the changes I ask for, it doesn't mean I walk away forever because something doesn't hold up to Christian standards. But it does mean I will continue to speak up, dig my heels in when necessary, and plant seeds of truth. The rest I leave to Him who can do "immeasurably more than all we ask or imagine" (Eph. 3:20).

Confidence Can Take Criticism

When I was on *The View*, I often heard from viewers about the way I composed myself on the show. They'd say, "Candace, how did you keep control of your temper? How do you stay gracious when others seem angry, bitter, and harsh?" It's true that as the token conservative on the panel, I took a lot of hits. But the fact is, conflict and criticism are part of life. Learning to withstand criticism is a necessity for any woman, especially if we choose a public life. The sooner we learn to respond with confidence, the better.

I guess I've always had my fair share of critics. As a

child actor attending public school, I was under the scrutiny of the media and of my peers. At times, I was picked on pretty mercilessly. But these days, my critics are mostly people who've seen me on TV. I'm criticized about my political views, about how I dress, about what I'm doing with my time, and about how I parent. People even track my social media posts and criticize my personal life, with comments like, "It looks like you haven't been with your family enough." Things can get pretty personal.

By now I'm used to this. I try not to let criticism penetrate my heart, and I hold some things very firmly, like my faith. Other things I hold on to thoughtfully, like my political views. The rest I let go of, as best I can. Sometimes a comment will really sting and I have to take time to sift through it, like you would with flour when you're baking. Then I try to take what's valuable, whatever I can learn from, and leave the rest behind. Often I find that I'm leaving all of it behind because there was no real substance to the criticism, just carelessness or viciousness.

Let's take a moment here to acknowledge a hard truth: women can be very mean to each other. We are sort of known for it, aren't we? Tearing each other down has become all too common. Some do it to make themselves feel better, often in the name of "constructive" feedback. The worst, in my opinion, is when this kind of criticism is done in a faith context—urging each other toward more "righteous" or "holy" behavior. Sisters, this kind of criticism can truly be offered or received only in the context of a personal relationship in which trust has been earned and is mutual.

I'm personally convicted that such criticism of one another must stop. We have to start turning the tide somewhere. Why not begin with you and me? We must stop the cycle of being mean to other women. I urge you to consider whether you're guilty of this yourself—of criticizing other women to their face, behind their back, or, more likely, via social media. Resolve right now that you will try to stop this behavior! Let's erase the stigma of being catty and cutthroat and become the women God made us to be: encouraging, confident, and graceful.

Our Ultimate Confidence

Ultimately, my confidence comes from knowing *whose* I am. My identity in Christ is secure whether I mess up or succeed, whether everyone thinks I'm great or very few do. Beyond that, my confidence will always be bolstered by three things: preparation, empathy, and open hands.

For me, feeling confident begins with prayer. I talk with God about what's happening or coming up, and I lift it up, offering it to Him. My prayer is that I'll be filled with equal measures of boldness *and* grace.

Then I practice. This is true whether I'm getting ready for filming, a race, or a hard conversation. I practice,

practice, practice! Here's where my training as an actress and an athlete makes a difference in the rest of my life. When I'm truly prepared, I feel ready for the inevitable twists and turns that come. Whenever you face a difficult situation or conversation, practice a gracious response. Like a student prepping for a test, you will gain confidence through practice. Time spent preparing is never time wasted.

Confidence Is Empathetic

Confidence knows how to read a room. We will always connect with others if we are empathetic, considering their needs before our own. Simply imagine what it's like to be the other person. Some people empathize easily, but some of us have to work at it. A good starting place for empathy is to remind yourself often of the *imago Dei*, the truth that every person you encounter is made in the image of God. That is the source of their worth. I try to give people the benefit of the doubt, knowing that I don't usually know the full story. Maybe they're not impatient with me, necessarily; they are simply preoccupied with something unrelated. Or maybe they're dealing with a deep grief or pain I know nothing about. This practice can help us extend grace and kindness in tangible ways. In my meeting with the producers, imagining how they perceived me helped me anticipate their response and gave me ideas on how best to approach them.

Confidence Doesn't Demand Control

Like it or not, we have limited control in this life. We control how we behave and how we think, and that's about it! Yes, we can handle those things to the best of our ability. Anything outside of that? Let it go. Here's where I lean heavily on the sovereignty of God. I say to myself, "He's got this" to remind myself that I don't have to.

The other thing about confidence through relinquishing control is, when you know your real purpose, you'll have clarity about where and when to delegate or let others drive. Remember my friend Shelene? She started Skip1 as a small nonprofit. It's now grown quite a bit. Shelene knows what she's good at and what she's not good at. She delegates accordingly. Does she have to do everything to feel confident? No way! If she tried, Skip1 wouldn't be able to do half the good they do!

A good rule for knowing when to let go and delegate is this: only do what only you can do. Then let others do the rest. In the example about my approaching the *Fuller House* executive producers, there was no way I was going to delegate that hard conversation to my manager or anyone else. I knew it was my conversation to have, even though it was going to be difficult. And at the same time, it wasn't my area of expertise to come up with the rewrites needed for the script. That's where I had to let them do what they do best.

Your Turn

The next time you're feeling anxious about something and need confidence, try to prepare, empathize, and relinquish control.

- **PREPARE.** Pray, collect your thoughts. If you don't have time to fully prepare, resist the urge to respond quickly. Take a beat. Breathe. Pause before you speak. Collect your words and self-edit before you dive in. Reacting on the fly, I've learned, is never a smart strategy. Preparation wins every time.

- **EMPATHIZE.** See people with respect and empathy. Remind yourself that every person is made in the image of God and is therefore worthy of dignity. Imagine how the people you're approaching might feel and what background they've come from. Know that they don't hold all the power in the room. You are each flawed and also uniquely loved by God.

- **RELINQUISH CONTROL.** Do what you reasonably can do, then let go of control. Leave the results to God. We can only do our part, which is to speak and act faithfully, as God has called us to do. But how people respond? That is outside of our control. We hope for the best, and we trust God with the outcome.

CHAPTER 9

My Best Friendship Advice

Kindness works to cultivate

meaningful relationships

Have you ever known someone who lived in one place their whole life, surrounded by an ever-growing family and lifelong friends? That seems so special to me. The character I play in the Aurora Teagarden Mysteries is like this; Aurora has lived her whole life in a town where everyone knows each other. It's a town of friends. However, if you've seen this mystery movie series, you know that some of these friends have been murdered, and one has been doing the killing. Yikes! And so the mystery begins. Good thing it's fiction!

For most of us, being surrounded by lifelong friends feels fictional too. For one of a million reasons, we've moved away from the place where we grew up, maybe for college or a job or a relationship. Maybe we've moved once, twice, or many times. Maybe you just haven't found the spot on the map where you can put down roots and make friends, or maybe it's your friends who are constantly moving away.

In my life, I've found myself in a new place several times, searching for new friendships and community. If you've been there and done that, you already know that this can be lonely work, but I've always found friends in the usual ways.

Friends from Work

Work friendships come easily to me. Maybe that's because ever since I was a child, my professional life has been a source of joy. When I'm working, I'm in my happy place. That makes it easy for me to bond with the people working alongside me. The cast of *Full House* and *Fuller House* have become my second family. We work, celebrate, and mourn together. When Jodie Sweetin went through a tough breakup recently, my heart broke for her. That friendship in particular is a lot like sisterhood. After all, she'll always be my little sis.

Not everyone loves their job like I do, and if you're not in your happy place, it's hard to create meaningful bonds with the people around you. There's no shame in this. You can be kind and classy in the workplace even if you're not creating lasting relationships there. It can be as simple as a bright smile and hello in the hallway or asking colleagues about their family lives or checking in to see how their day is going or who wants coffee if you're going for a coffee run.

Friends through Our Kids

Since Val and I have prioritized our family in a big way, our social life revolved around our kids as they were growing up. Some special friendships formed during that time of our lives. We don't see those people much now that the kids are grown, though. We've had to be deliberate in seeking out their company, and it can get tricky when the kids aren't close anymore. That said, I want our kids to realize that, as adults, we need friendships too. It's not all about the kids! I've said this more than once: the marriage is the center of the family, not the children.

Friends from Church

Many friendships are based on shared interests, so this one is important to me as a woman of faith. Worship services and Bible studies have brought many meaningful friendships into my life. Since these relationships usually have some sense of routine—Sunday worship, for instance—there is a consistency that helps create an expectation of community and a special bond. I love seeing the same faces through the years as I show up on Sundays. Because I so often travel for work, it means so much to be at my home church when I'm able.

But work, kids, and church have mostly provided *accidental* friendships, or friendships by proximity. When recently my best friend packed up to move to another state, I began to wonder if maybe I needed to invest in building new friendships the way I invest in my family and career, with the same intentionality and goal setting that are so much a part of my life in those other spheres.

Intentional Friendship

Sometimes the advice I give gets handed right back to me. Does that ever happen to you? It's like God uses the desires of my heart for the people I love to show me what He wants for me! I just love it when that happens. Like recently when I had a heart-to-heart with Natasha, encouraging her to invite new friends into her life, especially Christian friends to support her in her faith walk and to help her keep some accountability. Some friendships she had growing up have dropped off now that she's graduated. Some of her friends have moved away to go to college. Plus some friendships seemed to be costing her more, emotionally, than she was giving. I know firsthand the impact of healthy, nurturing friendships, and I want that for her, especially in this pivotal time.

After I shared my heart, Natasha's first question was, "Are you telling me I can't be friends with people who aren't Christians anymore?" I assured her my point was not that she should *abandon* any friends, though she might have to do some pruning, but that she needs to be deliberate about gathering new friends into her life.

She was surprised at that word pruning. I guess that's not a word teenage girls use often. What I love about my daughter is, she asks great questions. She wondered out loud what pruning her friendships looked like practically. I explained that I meant pruning like in a garden, when you trim back a plant that might otherwise take over everything.

Scripture has lots of gardening metaphors. John 15, for instance, describes God as the gardener who prunes the branches so that the garden can grow according to His good design. It sounds painful, but it's for our health and growth.

I told Natasha that I want her to cultivate friendships that will encourage her in her God-given purpose and help her reach her goals. I want her to cultivate the kind of company that will help her grow, and I want her to be exactly the same kind of friend to others. This might mean pruning back on some friendships, and it might mean starting out in search of some new ones as well.

Taking My Own Friendship Advice

As I reflected on that conversation, I realized I need to take my own advice and tend to my own garden. In the past few years, particularly during my time on *The View*, many of my friendships got put on hold. My time was so limited, and I was determined to preserve my family time at all costs, so what I'd call "conditional friendships" faded away. I wouldn't say those were fair-weather friends. It's just that these friendships were based on conditions that changed.

It's a natural part of adult life to let go of friendships,

and I'm grateful for the ebb and flow of those relationships, but now that I'm back home, taking stock of my
friendship garden, I've begun asking some critical questions for the next season.

- Who can I depend on outside of my family?
- Which friendships should I invest in when my time is
  limited?
- Who will stick with me when I need to take a break,
  so we can pick up where we left off, without missing
  a beat?
- Where do I still need to prune?

Proverbs 27:9 outlines a simple friendship goal. I love
the Message paraphrase of this verse: "A sweet friendship
refreshes the soul."

Lately I've been pausing to ask, "Who is this for me?"
I'm also taking some time to consider whether I am
refreshing the souls of other women. Mind if we ask those
questions together? Will you consider your friendship garden as I consider mine?

I've decided that when it comes to friendship, the goal
is to be surrounded by positive, hardworking, challenging
people—people who inspire me to be my best, kindest self!
As you think about your friendships, I'd love for you to
consider making that your goal too. And since the reason
I wrote this book is to raise the bar, challenging women

everywhere to elevate themselves and others by being classy and kind, consider me your first friend on the list!

Time to Prune

"She got in with the wrong crowd." As a parent, this sentence stirs up feelings of dread and anxiety for me. It's shorthand for what we all know intrinsically—that the company we keep is bound to bring either good consequences or bad ones. God's Word has been beating this drum for ages, stating, "Bad company corrupts good character" (1 Cor. 15:33).

On the contrary, good company inspires us to be our best selves. Again, Scripture confirms what we know in our guts. "Whoever walks with the wise becomes wise" (Prov. 13:20 ESV).

I'm viewing friends and potential new friends through this lens. Do they inspire me or belittle and compare? Are they positive or negative? Do they edify or do they gossip? Will I become wiser and more like Christ simply by being in their orbit? If not, maybe it's time to prune.

It's also good to remember that relationships are reciprocal. Doing good goes both ways, and ideally we take turns giving and receiving. I know in my own life there have been friends with whom it wasn't mutual enough to keep investing in the relationship. Maybe you have a friend in your life who, emotionally, makes more withdrawals than deposits. In that case, you might want to close the account and move on! It's simply not healthy.

Choosing Your Friends

God's Word has a lot to say about friendship! I was reminded today that "the righteous choose their friends carefully" (Prov. 12:26). That word choose communicates a lot. It's not just about who comes into your life; it's about who you *choose* to allow into your heart, who you *choose* to allow to speak into your life. That got me thinking about what characteristics I desire most in friendships. Here are my top six.

1. **I WANT FRIENDS WHO ARE KIND.** I'm drawn to people who show compassion. More and more, I'm learning that you can only extend grace when you've already received it from God. Then it's simply an overflow of His ultimate kindness. It creates a kind of contagious joy!

2. **I WANT FRIENDS WHO ARE STRONG.** In the song "Unbreakable Smile," Tori Kelly sings, "Don't mistake kindness for weakness." If you think about it, only the strong can truly be kind! Since life is bound to get hard at times, women who have that inner strength and resilience make good friends.

3. **I WANT FRIENDS WHO ARE LOYAL.** Once I let someone into my heart, I honor them and think the best of them. I

rush to offer help when they need it. They might not even know they need it! I desire this in friends as well.

4. **I WANT FRIENDS WHO ARE GENTLE.** Good friends help you be your best self, but we can't always be at our best! You might be snotty-nosed with tears, but a true friend will listen gently and help set your feet on the path to feeling better. They speak the truth in love, whether it's about your relationship or not. They don't criticize and tear you down. They give grace generously, just as they might hope to receive grace themselves on their worse days.

5. **I WANT FRIENDS WHO ARE ENCOURAGING.** In good times and bad, "a sweet friendship refreshes the soul" (Prov. 27:9 MSG). Whether it's a good day or your worst, a friendship should feel like a drink of water when you're thirsty! I want to walk away from a conversation with a friend revived and energized, not drained and down. We've all had those relationships that suck up more emotional energy than they bring; those are the ones it might be time to prune.

6. **I WANT FRIENDS WHO ARE PRINCIPLED.** People I trust with my heart should share my values. I especially look for a biblical worldview and a desire to know and understand God's Word. It's so easy to be pulled into the views of the world, because that's where we live; I think of that "slow fade" the Casting Crowns song talks about, leading to a worldly view. It often happens one small decision at a time. It makes such a difference when you have Jesus-loving

friends who are oriented to the Word of God and will pray with you. When we walk the path of faith together, we are stronger. I am very cautious about developing friendships with women whose influence will pull me from that path.

Loving People Who Have Different Values and Opinions

Having said that, do I think we should turn our backs on people who don't share our values or views? No way! My strong sense is that this is where kindness matters big! Listening with open minds and hearts to those whose opinions and beliefs differ from ours is so important. That's where we learn and grow and where we can shine the light of Christ.

Here is where I will tell you something that may surprise you. My best friend is not a Christian. Let me repeat that. My BFF is not a Christian. Some of you may be baffled by this. Dilini has been my best friend since we were fifteen, and she knows me better than anyone. We met in tenth grade when I transferred to a new school. She was assigned to me as my new student greeter, to show me around and answer any question I might have. We ended up having a few classes together and decided to study and do homework together.

At first, her parents were really skeptical about allowing her to come over to my house, since I was on TV.

They didn't know what my background was and what kind of influence I'd be on her, so when they finally said yes, her dad came over with her to have a chat with my dad. Our two dads ended up talking for a few hours, laughing and recognizing that our families were very similar. Our homes were less than five miles apart, and both of our families had lived in them for more than fifteen years. Both families were hardworking and prioritized family over everything.

Dilini was fun, smart, open, honest, down-to-earth, a bit naive like me when it came to boys, not into drinking or drugs, and beautiful. She was everyone's friend at school, and yet she was never a gossip or in a clique. She never made it a big deal that I was on TV, yet never dismissed it either; she simply took it as a matter of fact, which made me feel accepted just as I was.

Our friendship was about connection and having a trusted buddy to share everything with, no matter how similar or different. We told each other all our secrets and shared all our dreams and fears.

Although our family was Christian and Dilini and her family were Buddhist, our core values were very much the same. As we grew older, in our college years, our own beliefs and convictions rooted deeper into what each of us believed in, as opposed to what our families believed in for us.

We didn't agree on certain social and political issues,

but we never once argued over them. We talked about them, easily and openly like best friends do, and were always okay to agree to disagree at the end of the conversation, without taking it personally. We understood *why* the other came from their point of view, because we explained to each other why. We listened with empathy and compassion and a sense of reason, so it never became a source of conflict between us. We *wanted* to better understand each other, and while that does not always come easily, we've always made this a conscious effort out of care for each other. Dilini and I still feel the same way today, after more than twenty-five years of friendship, and our love only grows for each other every passing day.

The great thing about having friends who don't agree with you about everything is that it sharpens you, if you allow it to. When I have to explain my opinion, it forces me to dig deeper into the why of what I believe. It gives me the genuine gift of learning to answer for my beliefs and values, and the chance to go deeper into their rational support.

Do I believe something because it seems the most fair and reasonable, because it benefits me best, or because it's biblical? And if it is biblical, where does it say so in the Bible? And if it's not in the Bible, should I reconsider my viewpoint? Searching for the answers not only deepens a friendship because of the thought and time you've taken to look into an issue but also strengthens your own convictions with knowledge. And knowledge produces confidence.

As Christians, we are encouraged to "always be prepared to give an answer to everyone who asks you to give the reason for the hope that you have. But do this with gentleness and respect" (1 Peter 3:15). Doing our homework in advance readies us to respond with gracious boldness when the time comes to speak for our faith.

Of course, there are always challenges with theological differences, particularly when it comes to our closest friendships. People have often asked me, "If your best friend isn't a Christian, is it too weird or uncomfortable to share the gospel with her?" The answer is, "No way!" All the more, I desperately want to share it, and I have multiple times. But it isn't something I keep pushing to the front of every conversation. Only God can open a person's heart, and I trust in that with prayer.

It doesn't mean I don't talk about God or pepper my words with the language of faith, because this is such a big part of who I am. I continue to be myself, giving God glory, whether someone around me fully understands or not. What I hope everyone sees in me is the joy of Christ, and I hope I can help them be comfortable enough to ask questions that will open the door for more conversation about Him.

Many of my work friendships are with people whose beliefs are very different from my own, and I consider some of them my closest friends. What I like is that when you're talking with people you love, you genuinely want to listen and understand their point of view.

It also forces me to find where my own convictions are. Being married only once and to the same person for more than twenty years, I'm usually the one friends and coworkers come to for marriage advice. This is a good example of when I get sharpened, since I need to be prepared to explain why I believe my marriage has been successful because of a biblical worldview, when they may not know what that is. This opportunity for influence also stands as a reminder to myself to keep on walking the talk. The advice I have for my friends might be meant for them, but it's gold to my own heart and soul too.

In the same way, as I mentioned in a previous chapter, I work with many dear LGBT friends. My love for them compels me to understand their pain and oppression and their passion for fighting for equality, when I may not inherently understand what that feels like. Remember that having empathy and compassion doesn't mean you must agree on everything, but differences are never an excuse to be mean or dismissive, for either party.

Whether we disagree on politics, religion, family values, or parenting standards, we *always* have the opportunity to be kind. No matter what dividing lines fall between you and a colleague, friend, or family member, you can always demonstrate compassion while remaining true to your convictions. That's the beauty of gracious boldness!

Sometimes I wonder if that's why, in our culture, we have a difficulty with extending kindness. We've lost respect for people who don't think like us. When I read the Bible, it's clear to me that's not something Jesus would do. It certainly doesn't glorify God. How does marginalizing, excluding, or trivializing people communicate that they are made in His image?

We are all shaped by our experiences, and we each have had very different experiences. I don't know about you, but many of the most generous acts of kindness toward me have happened when someone chose to meet me in my own experience. When Whoopi knocked on my dressing room door to check on me, listen, and understand my fear. When Dilini understood my shame and regret for my poor behavior at my birthday party and chose to forgive me.

That's called empathy, and it's a cousin of kindness. Empathy is simply the practice of imagining how another person must feel, from their point of view. Instead of throwing our hands up in exasperation when we don't understand someone who is different from us, we see them through the eyes of love.

I think of it this way: You know the Golden Rule, right? Jesus authored it. In Matthew 7:12, He says, "Do to others what you would have them do to you." Empathy invites us to imagine ourselves in the shoes of another and then act with kindness toward them, just as we would most like to be treated ourselves.

Jesus' example offers us an invitation to open up, to listen, and to understand and even love people who believe differently than we do. In compassion and kindness, not with distaste and a readiness to argue. Just listen to understand where they're coming from.

I like to practice what's often called "active listening" when my friends are describing an experience I don't relate to. The goal of active listening is not to interject my personal beliefs or make judgments but to help a friend feel heard, which is always a gift. I might say, "Wow, that must be hard" or "Tell me more about that." Asking follow-up questions as well always helps people feel heard.

Friends, empathy is never wasted. Let's learn to extend it generously in our friendships, just as Jesus has so generously extended it to us.

Ask God to Expand Your Circle

God is a good provider. Sometimes I forget this and get nervous that I'm doing life all on my own. Looking back over my prayer journals, I can clearly see that He is always working to ensure that I have exactly what I need! Prayer didn't change God's mind or force Him to take care of me. He *wants* to take care of me, which includes providing great friends to love me and support me. Prayer reminds me how much I need Him and that I can't do this on my own. We were never meant to.

Philippians 4:6 is a reminder to pray. When we feel anxious about anything—our work, our finances, our health, our friendships—we can reach out to God through thankful prayer. I strive to put this verse into practice by thanking God and asking for what I need. Our part is simply to be alert and aware and keep our hands open for what He will provide!

As I was thinking about this chapter, Val and I went to church, and afterward we met a lovely woman and her daughter. While we were chitchatting, the husband and sons came over. It turned out that they have a farm and vineyard (so do we!), so we had lots in common. They were so kind and gracious. Afterward I said to Val, "I wonder if God wanted us to meet those people." We may never see them again, but for that moment I knew they were a gift to us, because of the simple joy we had in speaking with a family who shares some of the same joys, concerns, and values we do. Isn't that what friendship is really about?

Gather Your Girlfriends

When you find someone who brings out the best in you, cultivate that relationship. If you want to get to know someone better, you invest time in them. Create memories. Like I mentioned when we talked about hospitality, this doesn't have to be fancy or pretentious. Invite friends over for popcorn and a movie. Ask if you can bring some lawn games and meet them at the park. Keep it simple and make it a coffee date. The point is to get together and strengthen your connections, not to win some award for being the hostess with the mostest. It also helps to leave white space on your calendar so you can nurture friendships spontaneously. Like a well-watered plant in your garden, a relationship into which you've poured your time will grow.

There's nothing sweeter than time with girlfriends. And when we share a love for Jesus and for getting to know God's will for us through His Word? That's the best of all!

Don't you just love this promise from Matthew 18:20: "Where two or three gather in my name, there am I with them." When we gather together, Jesus always pulls up a seat at the table and joins us.

It's so easy to let our calendars fill up with work and obligations. If cultivating relationships matters, making time for them should be a priority too. Do you want to hear my personal goal? It's tough for me to cultivate relationships in travel seasons, but here's my plan and I'm sticking to it: I'm determined to have a friend date on my calendar once a month this year.

Practice the Simple Kindness of Checking In

Facetime is always fantastic, though, when some women I love and respect live far away. Investing in those relationships looks different than, say, cultivating relationships in my most intimate circle or my work friends or my Bible study group. Paul encouraged followers of Jesus to "encourage one another and build each other up" (1 Thess. 5:11). When there are miles between my friends and me, we live out this verse by texting and calling each other.

Karen Ehman is one of those people in my life. We met through mutual blogger friends, and we couldn't have more different lives. She lives in snowy Michigan and is a writer, speaker, and full-time mom. I live in sunny California and work mostly as an actress. We have the full-time mom part in common, I guess. Every mom is working full-time to care for her kids, right?

I know God brought Karen into my life. I've only seen her in person maybe half a dozen times, but she's one of my go-to buddies I chat with online or text. She prays for me all the time, and her messages to encourage me always come at the right time. She sends me simple messages like, "You've been on my heart, so I'm checking in." Karen knows her Bible, so I can call on her when I need advice on what God's Word says about a certain subject. She's been an encourager and cheerleader through some truly dark hours. She's such a gift! I laugh because I rarely see her, and yet she's become a flourishing part of my friendship garden. She is such a strong warrior woman in my life. I am praying that God gives me many more friends like Karen and provides me with opportunities to be this kind of friend to others. What a gift!

The Ultimate Friend

Trusting others.

Making emotional investments.

Sticking with each other through thick and thin.

Keeping confidences.

These friendship essentials often don't come as easily to adults as they did when we were children. We all want to protect ourselves and have to be careful of what we share with whom. Because of the fame factor in my life, I feel extra cautious. I never want to read something I shared in confidence on social media or in a gossip column. I can usually discern over time whom I can trust, but I can't always be as open and honest, because my heart has had to be guarded to some extent. I've been burned in the past, both intentionally and unintentionally. Unintentionally is always worse, because you know the person didn't mean to, but it can leave you feeling exposed and can be damaging and hurtful nevertheless. Either way, you look at things more closely and you pay attention to the signs, which I've learned over the years because they become obvious. But you know what? Sometimes I need to be okay with just sharing things with God. He is enough for me. He will bring me what I need, but ultimately what I really need is His presence.

Don't you just love this promise, found in Psalm 25:14: "The friendship of the LORD is for those who fear him, and he makes known to them his covenant" (ESV).

I can't say that my human mind can fully wrap itself around this, but I do know that God is my friend. He knows me better than anyone else does. He even knows me better than I know myself. He is the best friend a girl can have, and in seasons of loneliness it is clear to me that He is the only friend I truly need. He longs to be your best friend too. Other friends will come and go. Friendship is marked by seasons. But not with Jesus; His love for you is everlasting. He is a friend you can always count on.

Your Turn

As you take stock of your friendship garden, which friendships refresh your soul? How can you nurture those friendships in the next week, the next month, the next year? Maybe start by reaching out to those friends as soon as you finish this chapter. Give them a call, shoot them a text, or write them a note, letting them know how much they mean to you.

I'll go first. I'm going to call my friend Karen and read the words I wrote about her in this chapter. (Even though I know she will read them as soon as this book hits the shelves. She's *that* kind of friend!) I'd rather that she hear it straight from my heart to hers.

Then imagine that the conversation I had with Natasha is really a conversation I'm having with you. How can you nurture healthy, life-giving friendships? Here are the steps I'd encourage you to take.

- **PRUNE.** Are there any friendships in your life that are like an unwieldy plant that takes up too much time or energy? How might you guard against that? How might you set up some new boundaries that still communicate care yet protect your time and energy as well?

- **CHOOSE.** What characteristics do you most desire in friends? Make a wish list! How might you seek out such friendships? How might you better cultivate these same qualities in yourself? Take a step this week!

- **PRAY.** Thank God for the friendships you have now and have had in the past. Ask God to lead you into relationships that will be a mutual blessing.

- **GATHER.** Make time to talk with a friend in person this week, even if you meet for only a few minutes.

- **ENCOURAGE.** Take the time to encourage one friend this week. A note or a text is easy enough. Neither takes very long, but they both have the potential to make a big difference. Let a friend know why you're glad she's in your life and how you see her living out her purpose with grace.

CHAPTER 10

Sending Out the Bat-Signal

Kindness starts small and
trusts every action matters

As I write this final chapter, Hurricane Harvey has just slammed into Texas, dumping more than forty inches of rain and leaving the city of Houston underwater. Like you, my family and I have stared at the images of this catastrophe on our phones and television screen with our eyes wide and our hands covering our mouths. We can't help but wonder, "What can we possibly do to help?"

Hurricanes are just the beginning. From my hometown in sunny California, across the country, and around the globe, people are hurting. The rhetoric in the public sphere is increasingly angry. Personal and collective tragedies are the norm, not the exception.

With so many displaced and suffering, the needs feel overwhelming. We all want to shake our heads and ask, "What can we possibly do to help?" Simply being kind and classy may not feel like enough in the face of such very real, deep needs. Can it really make a difference?

Ask Crystal and Trey, Houstonians who rescued twenty-two people in their kayak after the floodwaters hit.

Ask Aaron, another resident who rescued a stranded

dog named Cash, found his owners on social media, and delivered him back once the hurricane was over.

Ask the young man who carried his elderly neighbor upstairs to escape the flooding.[1]

Ask the Red Cross volunteers who handed out blankets and pillows to residents looking for a soft place to land in the storm.

Or the neighbors who offered encouragement and support to each other as they rode out the hurricane.

It may not be what we see on the news or read in our social media feeds, but in moments of chaos and moments of calm, when the storm hits or when life feels like a perfect day at the beach, kindness makes all the difference in the world.

The Women I Admire Most

In the introduction, I mentioned some examples of trailblazing women who inspire me. Women like Harriet Tubman, Amelia Earhart, and Marie Curie. Some of my favorite women are famous, and you'll find their names in history books.

But many are not. Some of them are famous simply in my eyes because they are the women closest to me who display the ultimate in kindness to others.

....

1   Laura Vitto, "Houston's Good Samaritans Are Watching Out for Each Other As Harvey Rages On," *Mashable* (August 27, 2017), *http://mashable.com/2017/08/27/harvey-houston-good-samaritans/ #w5jjWYA8wOqE.*

Women like my mom, Barbara, who has always been there for her children, takes care of my grandma every day, and talks online with people she's never met to help them through especially difficult times.

Women like my friend Shelene, who switched careers at the height of hers to help those less fortunate.

Nurses and caretakers who spend endless amounts of energy tending to and loving on the elderly and children in hospitals.

The barista at my regular coffee shop who says, "Have a blessed day, Candace" with a warm smile every time I pick up my order.

In ways big and small, ordinary and extraordinary, these are women who are graciously bold in caring for others and extending kindness to the world around them.

I want to follow their lead and legacy.

What about you? Who's on your list of role model women? If you could have dinner with any women—from any era of history—who would you choose?

I'll take a wild guess that they'd all be lovely guests. They're probably not the women who are pushy, rude, or condescending. I doubt you are drawn to the kind of women who are angry or antagonistic or who use their voice to make other people feel small.

Sure, success is a great thing. Hard work is admirable. Good looks can leave quite an impression. Praise and applause can feel great. But ultimately, such trophies gather dust and end up in the closet. I don't know about you, but I want more than that.

In my industry, and living in LA, we all have celebrity encounter stories. And every time I talk to someone about meeting a celebrity, the first thing they remember and talk about is whether that person was nice. The celebrity could be the most beautiful, the biggest name, or from an all-time favorite team or band, but if he or she doesn't seem authentic and kind, that becomes their lasting memory.

It's funny, when you stop to consider things we commonly chase after in this life, and stack those up against what people are most likely to remember about us. I am willing to bet that we will not be remembered for our social media likes, performance reviews, clean house, on-trend hairstyle, or perfect family photo Christmas cards sent out miraculously on time.

No, what we'll be remembered for is the way we treated people around us.

It's *kindness* that has the power to live on through the ages.

Maybe the women on your list have never won a Nobel Prize or an Academy Award, but they've impacted you, simply by considering your needs above their own. Truly, the most inspiring women I know are queens of kindness!

There is no greater elegance than a woman who chooses to think of others before herself. When we live by the Golden Rule, *we* start to sparkle! Treating people with care and compassion, as they would most wish to be treated, is what makes a woman truly classy. And that kind of class is timeless.

When the people around me think of the words kind and classy, I hope they'll equate those words with me. And I bet you feel the same way.

The Ripple Effect

Here's the kicker. Kindness almost always starts small. And it *always* grows from there.

When we choose to be kind, there is always a ripple effect. Like a rock thrown into the ocean, kindness spreads in ever-growing circles of impact.

So go ahead and start small.

Let's do an experiment. What would happen if today you decided to be kinder to yourself? What if you woke up and silenced the voices in your head that said you didn't do enough yesterday and will probably fail again today? What if you spoke words of kindness to yourself instead, looked yourself square in the eye in the mirror, and reminded yourself that you are a beloved and chosen daughter of God? What if you ate the kinds of foods that make your body feel fueled for the tasks ahead, rather than filling it with junk that makes you feel guilty and sluggish? Or wore an outfit that makes you feel like a million bucks, and spent a few extra minutes on your hair and makeup?

What could it hurt to choose to let your outside match your inside? How would that boost of confidence impact the way you treat the people around you?

What if you decided to start being more kind to the people who live behind your front door? Or bought your husband his favorite coffee just because, or said yes even when you have a headache or are too tired? (It will actually help—wink.) What if you take your kids to the park this afternoon? When someone leaves toothpaste squished in the sink or leaves the garage door open for the hundredth time, what if instead of reacting in the heat of the moment, you took a beat, prayed for self-control, and responded with kindness?

What might change in your neighborhood as a result of a single kind act? Could you and your kids give away lemonade and cookies for free on the front lawn? Could you weed someone's flowerbeds anonymously? Could you take in your next-door neighbor's garbage cans too? Could you invite everyone to a backyard barbecue at your house? It might not change the world, but it sure could make someone's day.

Let's keep following the ripples.

How could it impact your community if you made a concentrated effort to be kind, even when others aren't? I believe we all have the capacity to make a difference in our day-to-day lives, simply by responding graciously when someone else is rude.

Could you elevate the conversation online with kind

remarks instead of snarky ones? When someone posts an insult, could you offer a blessing in return? What if we decided to always respond to human suffering with acts of kindness? Sure, suffering will come, but could we bear it more easily if we shared the load?

I admit that this is not a book about how to achieve world peace, but it is a book for how to have more peace in your own heart, your own relationships, your own home. Why not start where you are?

Be kind to yourself, because you are deeply loved. Be kind to others, because they are loved too. Being kind begins with extending grace, not only to others but to yourself. Start there. It won't solve everything, but kindness—no matter how small—is never wasted. You will never regret being kind, and you can trust that even if you don't see its effects today, your actions are rippling outward to make a difference.

Sending Out the Bat-Signal

Any Batman fans out there? Do you remember how the citizens of Gotham alerted Batman that they were in need? They sent out the Bat-Signal, illuminating the darkness with the bright symbol of their hope, as a sign for their hero to come help them. That's what this book is. I'd like to send out a kindness light, as a symbol of my hope in all of you, and a signal for us all to get to work.

Like the crime-ridden streets of Gotham, this planet is a mess. I live in the real world just like you. I know that the news is scary, our relationships are messy, and kindness seems to be on the endangered species list. But I have great hope. I believe it is possible for us to carry ourselves with grace and dignity, even in a culture that seems to celebrate anger and division. I have a deep desire to raise up an army of kind and classy women to impact all we come into contact with, and in turn the world.

These are the kinds of everyday heroes I think our world needs more of. And here's where I hope you'll hear me. You don't need a cape to become this kind of hero. You don't need unique influence, advanced education, or special technology. This isn't a job exclusively for the experts among us. In fact, all amateurs welcome!

There's only one requirement to be a kindness hero: that you're willing. All you have to do is show up, start small, and keep at it.

But before you enlist, let me give this disclaimer: we cannot do this on our own.

In-Powered versus Empowered

I'm a firm believer that there's a difference between being an empowered woman and being one who is in-powered by the Holy Spirit. This is not a pep talk. I'm not giving you a list of feel-good mantras to ramp up your confidence in your own abilities.

But I am going to encourage you to remember *whose* you are and where your true strength and ability come from.

If Christ isn't the source of our actions toward each other, even the decision to be kind will always come from a selfish, me-focused, "my rights" sort of attitude. We will be kind toward others, expecting them to always be kind to us and likely getting our feelings hurt when they don't. This doesn't change a thing. It's the opposite of the mission I hope to accomplish.

Here's a snapshot of what we're trying to stay away from: "We ourselves were once foolish, disobedient, led astray, slaves to various passions and pleasures, passing our days in malice and envy, hated by others and hating one another" (Titus 3:3 ESV).

Kindness has to be learned. It does not come naturally to our sinful nature, which demands a me-first mentality. Because of the damage done by sin, we can't love others well on our own, but that's only part of the story. And the good part comes next. "But when the *goodness and loving kindness* of God our Savior appeared, he saved us, not because of works done by us in righteousness, but according to his own mercy, by the washing of regeneration and renewal of the Holy Spirit" (vv. 4–5 ESV, emphasis mine).

Though we did not deserve it, Jesus responded to us with goodness and kindness. He is the ultimate example of graciousness. How humbling! We can respond to others with kindness because we've received kindness ourselves—and not just any kindness but the most extravagant display of kindness known in human history!

That's just how loved we are. And we start living lives of kindness and purpose when we realize that's how much God loves those around us too.

This is where the Spirit of God invites us to move from a me-first mentality into a faith-first mentality. We need God's help to see the people around us as the image bearers they are.

We don't need to be empowered with a long list of dos and don'ts for how to treat each other. A rah-rah pep talk won't be enough for so high a calling. Rather we need to be in-powered by the Holy Spirit to see everyone through the eyes of love. No exceptions. Your husband, your best friend, your pastor. As well as the grouchy cashier, the silent strangers in the elevator, the real men and women hiding behind avatars on Facebook, the mailman. God's love is fierce and passionate for them all.

When we live our lives submitted to His plan for us, passionately pursuing our mission to bring Him glory, He will take our small acts of kindness and multiply them in ways we cannot imagine. Have you noticed that kindness is contagious? Sometimes all it takes is a cheerful customer service rep or a whistling stranger on the subway to turn our day around. Who knows who will be inspired to treat others well because of your example! Trust the ripple effect. Believe it. And do your part.

Be You and Be Kind

I was recently asked to participate on the celebrity panel of the game show *To Tell the Truth*. I sat alongside celebrities Oliver Hudson, Kal Penn, and Ross Mathews, and we were presented with three people who all claimed to be the same person with the same talent, job, or incredible achievement. One of them had to be honest; the other two didn't. It was our job to ask the participants questions before deciding who we thought was telling the truth.

In addition to host Anthony Anderson, there was his brassy mom, Doris, the official scorekeeper, who chimed in with unfiltered comments, asked the panel her own questions, and tried to embarrass her son as a part of her act.

During that episode, I was the unlucky one to get most of Mama Doris's attention. As I was asking my questions to the participants, Mama interjected, telling Anthony, "Move on; she's stupid. She's got dumb questions."

I was stunned. Did I just hear what I thought I heard? I leaned over to Oliver and asked, "Did she just call me stupid? Did I hear that right?" I was flabbergasted.

Oliver kind of chuckled, because he was just as shocked. "Yup."

Certainly, I've dealt with these kinds of comments on social media, but never before have I been so directly insulted to my face. Not only that, but this was on television, in front of a live audience!

My mind raced to think of a rebuttal, something that would put her in her place. I was waiting for the next round to get back at her, when my conscience came over me.

"Kindness, Candace. Kindness always wins," a gentle whisper spoke in my spirit. I didn't want to appear weak by not saying anything back, and the truth was, I was boiling inside. I felt humiliated and I was angry. Everyone tells me I have a great sense of humor, but I found nothing funny about her belittling comment. I wrestled to know how to respond, wanting to lash back and have the last word, while also knowing that it would be a poor choice to lower myself to her level. I knew my integrity was worth more than that.

When it was time for me to ask a follow-up question, I admitted openly that I couldn't think of another question because I was still stunned that Mama Doris called me stupid. Mama shot back that if it bothered me that much, I should have come back at her if I had the guts.

"I don't play that way," I told her. "It's not my style, and it never will be. So why don't you be you, and I'll be me."

Then, growing in courage, I realized I had the floor, and I decided I was going to use it for good. So I told her that I forgave her for calling me stupid, because Jesus forgave me first, and I walked over to her and gave her a hug.

I'll admit, it was kind of awkward, and I was a bit uneasy afterward, but Mama Doris never came after me again. In fact, she backed me up for the rest of the show.

After we finished taping, Doris approached me. She wanted me to know that her defiant attitude was her shtick on the show, and she didn't think I'd be offended. She said she didn't think anything could rattle me after being on *The View*, so she went for it. Mama Doris was right in that nothing could get me to attack back. Not then and not now. But it didn't mean I didn't want to. As she walked away, she told me she was proud of me. She passed a colleague, pointed back at me, and said simply, "I like that girl."

Kindness is a choice. Sometimes it's an easy one to make, and we reap immediate benefits. Other times it's one of the hardest choices you'll ever make, and extending grace to someone who has hurt you or riled you will go against everything your heart is telling you.

My advice? Choose it anyway. Your life won't change overnight. I've learned these lessons about living graciously over the course of many years. And God isn't done with me yet! I still have a lot to learn about how to live in a way that always glorifies Him. I'm so grateful He's still working on me, teaching me how to respond to others like He does. I hope to perpetually be a student in the school of kindness.

Your Turn

I'm excited to hear about the work God does in your life as you rise to the challenge to live your life for Him. That may feel like a big calling (it is!), but we live and love like Jesus with one act of kindness at a time. As you close this book, I hope you'll take the next right step today and choose just one way to be kind. Then another. Then another. Then another.

Here's a few ideas to get you started. Write a thank-you note. Extend an invitation. Bring muffins to the office. Offer someone a ride to the airport. Donate blood. Challenge yourself to go a day without saying anything negative. Call your grandmother. Look at the month ahead for birthdays and plan something special for a friend or family member. Send a care package. Send congrats flowers for a friend who reached a new milestone. Make a double batch of soup and bring half to someone who just moved. Wave at kids on a school bus.

Kindness is a chance for us to get creative at doing good in a world that needs it! So let's have fun with it.

Kindness is so countercultural that it will take practice. But day by day, step by step, these small actions will become more than isolated, every-now-and-then events.

All that practice adds up to become a *lifestyle*. When you choose kindness over rudeness, when you choose serving others above yourself, your brain will be rewired into a whole new way of living. Time and practice will help these habits become second nature. With God's help, you will be in-powered to make a statement with your very life, declaring that kindness, compassion, empathy, and gentleness are timeless in beauty and powerful to transform.

As I was working on this book, I received an email from a friend. She wrote, "One final piece of encouragement related to in-powerment. Knowing you were working on the book, I'd been praying for you throughout the day. Tonight, as I was packing a box (moving tomorrow), God interrupted my thoughts and gave me a phrase from a Scripture—'immeasurably more.' I sensed it was for you—your face popped into my mind as He repeated that phrase a few times. So just wanted to encourage you as you write that God is going to do immeasurably more than all you ask or imagine according to His power that is at work within you!"

Maybe you've read the passage she mentioned. It is Ephesians 3:20–21, and it feels like a fitting place to end our conversation.

"Now to him who is able to do immeasurably more than all we ask or imagine, according to his power that is at work within us, to him be glory in the church and in Christ Jesus throughout all generations, for ever and ever! Amen."

APPENDIX 1

My Story

Sometimes, especially when I'm not *feeling* charitable, I challenge myself to do a random act of kindness. Maybe I'll slip a homeless person a few bills, offer a compliment to a stranger, or skip something for myself and pass it along to someone who needs it. Doing so never fails to make me smile. It always helps me walk with a little more spring in my step. It's my way of paying forward a tiny droplet from God's amazing ocean of grace and kindness.

It stuns me to think of what God did for me. In Him, I've found the ultimate kindness, freedom, and everlasting peace. His kindness inspires me to share my own story. Truly, the ultimate kindness we can show others is pretty simple: it's sharing Jesus. I want everyone to know God's kindness to me and for all of us. He is the truth that set me free. Here's my own story of accepting His radical love.

My Testimony

A lot of people think I was raised in a Christian home, maybe because my brother, Kirk, is a pretty public figure in Christian faith. But the truth is, we didn't grow up in a home where we talked about Jesus. My mom was a believer, but my dad didn't believe in God, and he didn't want religion taught in our home. He asked my mom not to discuss religion. He said if we wanted to pursue it on our own, we could decide that when we were older. So I didn't grow up in a Christian household, but I did grow up in a very moral home. Our parents taught us the difference between right and wrong. They taught us to live by the Golden Rule—to treat people the way you'd like to be treated—and I was a respectful, obedient child.

New to the Christian Faith

The first time I went to church, I was twelve years old. My parents were going through a difficult time in their marriage and were considering a divorce. A friend invited our family to church, hoping it might help my parents work out their problems. I remember that first time we drove to church. Dad hadn't told us where we were going. He just told us to get in the car. I looked around when we got there and thought, "Wow, this marriage crisis must be serious if my dad is willing to go to church!" I didn't know a thing about God or Jesus, and I just sat there with my sisters. Honestly, I felt pretty uncomfortable. I didn't know what "those people" were talking about. It was as if they were speaking a different language. We continued to go to that church week after week. Though I didn't immediately grasp everything about this new Christianity thing, I really liked the people there. They seemed genuinely kind and caring and joyful. It seemed to me that this Jesus they all loved was what distinguished them from other people I'd encountered. One Sunday when the pastor asked if anyone would like to ask Jesus into their heart, I raised my hand. I bowed my head and said the Sinner's Prayer and received Christ as my Savior. A few weeks later I was baptized with my brother and a couple other family members. I was very excited about my Christian life! It was so special to begin learning about Jesus and about my newfound faith. I could tell it was the beginning of a lifelong journey.

At the same time, I had been working on *Full House* for about two years, and the show was gaining popularity. I was going to school full-time and working on the show. On weekends, I traveled for publicity. I'd do press interviews and huge public appearances at malls and civic arenas. I had a happy and very busy life. At home, my parents continued working through their marital problems and decided to stay together. We had a happy, stable home life.

Because of this busy lifestyle, though, even though I had accepted Jesus into my heart, my teenage years didn't involve much church or faith practice. I went to church when I could, when I "had time," but it wasn't a priority. I remember thinking, "I can talk to God anytime. He lives inside my heart. I don't really need to go to church." This outlook soon became my habit. I'd talk to God just on my own, sending up thanks or asking for help here and there. Frankly, it wasn't much of a relationship, more of a help line. I made requests and put in effort when it was convenient for me, but I didn't do much listening. If this had been a human friendship, I would have encouraged God to do some serious pruning! I'm so glad He didn't.

By the time I was eighteen, I had moved out on my own. I wasn't financially dependent on my family anymore. I was free to do pretty much anything I wanted. Still, I wasn't the typical child star. I didn't get addicted to drugs or abuse alcohol or get into trouble with the law. I was a pretty responsible person. I liked being a good kid, and I liked pleasing my parents. I was the kind of girl who still called home when she got in for the night to let her mom and dad know she was safe. For me, a good day was when the director came over when we were finished and said, "Great job today, Candace." God wired me to be motivated to please others. So getting into trouble was never a real temptation.

Even so, I felt like my teen years were supposed to be a little rebellious. There must be some kind of testing the waters, right? At least, that's how I saw it at the time. I felt that maybe I should try some things my parents had told me were wrong. I looked around to see what other people my age were doing, and it seemed like my life was so tame by comparison. "If the worst thing I'm doing is being intimate with my boyfriend before marriage, I'm doing pretty good," I reasoned. "I'm pretty much a saint by comparison."

When I felt a tinge of conviction, I'd focus on the things I was doing that were good—things that maybe balanced the scales in my favor and made me a good person. When I thought about my good deeds, I could think of a lot. After all, I was involved in plenty of charity work, investing time and making other people's lives better. I could easily talk myself into feeling really good about myself.

If that didn't work, when I felt my conscience tug at me, I'd remind myself that God is a loving, forgiving God. I'd rationalize, "I can just ask for forgiveness!" When I did something I knew was wrong, I knew God wouldn't be pleased, so I'd pray, "God, would you please forgive me?" Then I'd get back to my good little life, doing my best to live morally.

I remember thinking, "Is this really how God works? I mean, I know God is a forgiving God. I know He is patient, but this is pretty easy! I can just do whatever I want. When I mess up occasionally, I just ask for forgiveness." It seemed too good to be true, and clearly it was convenient for me. I felt like I was living a pretty good life. If God was judging me according to the good works in my life, I figured He would give me a passing grade, if not an A+.

But my little tossed-up apologies weren't really repentance. Through His Word, and because of His extravagant grace, God helped me understand that repentance is a kind of sorrow that leads to lasting change. My occasional "sorry" was empty of real meaning, because I had no intention of making a change.

When the Dominoes Started to Fall

I wasn't convinced I needed to change anything, really, until my sister-in-law Chelsea introduced me to the novel *Left Behind* by Tim LaHaye and Jerry Jenkins. I saw my own ideas reflected in the character of Pastor Bruce Barnes, who was frighteningly one of those left behind! I had given my life to Christ. I called myself a Christian, but I wasn't producing fruit. I'd been using the promise of God's forgiveness as a license to live my life on my own terms rather than as His child. I cared more about my happiness than about my holiness. That book raised all kinds of questions in me. It was like the first domino in a series to fall. I wanted to know more. For the first time, I really wanted to know what God says. I opened my Bible, but it looked like a foreign language to me.

The next domino fell when my brother gave me a book that he said had rocked his world. He told me he hoped I'd read it too. I knew my brother was walking with God, and frankly we all thought he was a little weird. None of us quite got it yet. When he said this book had shown him something in the gospel that he'd never seen before, I was interested. Besides, when your older brother asks you to do something, you usually *want* to do it. I picked up *The Way of the Master* and started reading. I learned a lot through that book and realized how sinful I was. It helped me see that I'd been viewing my sin all wrong. I'd been comparing my sin with the standard of the world, thinking of myself as pretty holy compared with everyone else. Suddenly I realized that the standard for holiness isn't the world; it's the holiness of God. Compared with God, I'm not holy at all. None of my good deeds could change that. I finally saw that by God's standards, I fall far short of holiness!

Still, I thought, "Would a kind God really send me to hell?"

Another domino fell when I read this analogy:

Imagine there's a man guilty of murder standing in a court. The evidence is stacked against him.

The judge says, "What do you have to say for yourself?"

The murderer says, "I'm guilty and I'm truly sorry for my crime. I know you to be a kind judge. Can I please go free?"

No matter how compassionate, a good and just judge must sentence the man to a penalty. The judge would say, "It's good you are repentant, but you must be punished."

Check out 1 Corinthians 6:9: "Do you not know that the unrighteous will not inherit the kingdom of God?" (ESV).

As I studied this verse and others like it, I saw the true character of God for the first time. Yes, He's forgiving, but He is also a holy God and a just judge. I'd said I would follow God, but I'd conveniently left out the part of faith that was inconvenient for me.

I was convicted.

What was I supposed to do? That's where the good news of Jesus comes in! God isn't just a righteous and holy judge. He's also a merciful and loving God. He is both. He's just and forgiving, holy and loving, my Creator and my very best friend. And because He's the ultimate gentleman, never forcing us to submit to Him, He is also classy and kind.

In the ultimate act of kindness, He sent His one and only Son Jesus for us. Jesus lived a blameless life, never disobeying the Father. I tried to balance the scales in God's mind by doing enough good deeds to counteract my bad; Jesus never did a single thing wrong. He lived a sinless, guiltless life. Talk about tilting the scales!

Imagine that it's me standing in front of that judge. I am guilty. I have sinned and I am truly sorry. Just as I'm about to be sentenced to death, I find out that the most severe penalty has already been paid for me. Yes, I deserved hell. It is a place reserved for those who cannot attain the holiness of God. But Christ took my punishment for me. I felt sorrow—godly sorrow—for what I'd done. That sorrow led to a real repentance. Real repentance always turns into action. I suddenly wanted to turn 180 degrees away from my sin.

The Fruits of Repentance

Out of utter gratitude for all that Jesus has done for me, I *want* to live a life of service to Him. It's no longer about pleasing others. My desire is to please God! My deep desire is to hear God's words, "Well done, good and faithful servant!" (Matt. 25:23) spoken about *me*. I realize I'm not going to be perfect (that's why I need Jesus so much), but I ask God to help me die daily to my desire for sin. I no longer dive into my sin with the thought that I can simply ask for forgiveness. Will I sin again? Of course I will. I'm a human being. That comes with a natural gravitation toward rebellion and sin. But when I read this promise in Ezekiel, I hear my own name in God's pronouncement: "[Candace,] I will give you a new heart and put a new spirit in you; I will remove from you your heart of stone and give you a heart of flesh" (36:26). God did exactly that! He gave me a spiritual heart transplant, taking out my sinful, selfish heart and giving me a heart more like His. He also gave me a newfound freedom and changed my life in so many ways, including changing my desires and my priorities.

My hope for you is that you realize you can't live up to God's standards of holiness either. You've broken His law and rebelled against Him. You may feel a weight on your shoulders, but know that you too can be free. Although you can't live up to the law, you can be free from the punishment. Jesus took it already. You can embrace this freedom and peace in Christ too.

How to Study the Bible

Several times throughout this book, I mention studying the Bible. That may feel like a daunting task. I get it! With sixty-six books written by forty different authors over a span of thousands of years, the Bible is no ordinary book. Not to mention it is the very Word of God. I understand it can be intimidating.

However, God's Word has changed me from the inside out. It is through the Bible that I've learned who God is. It's also through the Bible that I've learned the truth about who *I* am—a cherished child of the King.

I'm not a Bible scholar. I've never been to Bible college, and yet over time, God's Word has become more and more familiar to me. It feels accessible even in the midst of my busy life. I want it to feel accessible to you too, whether you've been reading the Bible for decades or it's all new to you. Here are a few of my favorite ways to study the Bible that you might love too!

JOIN A WOMEN'S BIBLE STUDY. There is something about the encouragement of other women that helps me like nothing else to stick with studying God's Word. I've been involved in women's Bible studies for many years, and I've learned so much as a result. Ask your church about any women's Bible study options they may already have, or gather a group of close friends, pick a study, and dig in together.

A few of my favorite studies are:

Seamless: Understanding the Bible as One Complete Story by Angie Smith

Redeemed: Grace to Live Every Day Better Than Before by Angela Thomas-Pharr

Daniel: Lives of Integrity, Words of Prophesy by Beth Moore

Gideon: Your Weakness, God's Strength by Priscilla Shirer

JOURNAL. Just like I use my journal to record my prayers, I also use it to track what I am learning in God's Word. Write down verses or phrases that jump out at you, make lists of themes you see repeated in Scripture, or even write down questions that come up as you study. I bet you kept notes in school to help you learn. Journaling applies that same method to the study of God's Word.

ANNOTATE. *Annotate* is just a fancy word for "add notes to." You can keep a separate journal to track your Bible study, but you can also write right in the pages of your Bible. The purpose of your Bible is to help you discover who God is, not to be preserved for a museum display. Underline, highlight, even draw on the pages of your Bible to help you stick with your study.

Speaking of sticking with it . . .

PARK YOURSELF. Increasingly, we struggle to focus on one thing for a prolonged period of time. I often feel this when I am trying to dig into God's Word. I have to fight the temptation to keep checking things on my phone while I am studying or even to jump around in God's Word if something is hard to understand. Pick a book of the Bible and stick with it. You will learn so much more if you can force yourself to park and focus.

TAKE IT WITH YOU. Technology may have its drawbacks, but it can also be a huge help as we seek to get more of God's Word into our daily lives. Get a Bible app on your phone and read when you have some downtime. I often use my time in the hair and makeup chair to read the Bible on the YouVersion Bible app.

LET GO OF PERFECT. Often I hear from women who do not read the Bible because they have a picture-perfect, though totally unrealistic, view of Bible study in their heads. You don't have to wait until your house is quiet, your cup of coffee is steaming, and you feel ready to fully understand everything you read. That scenario will likely never happen. Just open your Bible and ask God to show you what He wants you to know.

PRAY. Before I start to study the Bible or read a devotional, I pray. I ask God to reveal to me what He wants me to learn, do, or ask for. I talk to Him, as in a real-life conversation, even out loud at times. "God, I don't understand this. What do you mean by this? God, can you explain this to me in another way? God, can you give me a practical example of this in my life?" These are all questions that help me tremendously, ones I'm not afraid to ask. Praying doesn't mean you need to be in a quiet corner either. I talk to Him in the car, waiting in the carpool line, if that's where I'm getting my study time in. Praying is conversation. Don't be afraid to talk to God while you're studying His Word.

There is no right way to study God's Word. Find a method of study that works well for you, and stick with it. You will be amazed at how God will transform your heart and your life through regular study of His Word.

Nurture Yourself

Body, Style, and Soul

Go behind the scenes with Candace Cameron Bure as she shares one hundred tips and tricks for feeling your best—both inside and out.

Available at Bookstores Everywhere

ZONDERVAN®
.com

Candace Center Stage

Candace Cameron Bure

Candace Center Stage, written by Candace Cameron Bure, *New York Times* bestselling author and star of the hit TV series *Full House* and *Fuller House*, tells the story of a little girl who loves to dance. But when her mother signs her up for ballet lessons, Candace quickly realizes she's no ballerina. As she moves and grooves across the floor, she topples all the ballerinas in her path. Her teacher, Miss Grace, tries to teach her proper ballet positions, but Candace is more interested in shakes and shimmies than in *plies* and *pas de bourrees*. On show night, Candace's tutu is tailored and her bun is beautiful, but her tummy is a rumbly mess. When disaster strikes onstage, Candace steps up and saves the day by doing what she does best—being Candace.

This adorable book sparkles and shines with a cover that includes embossing and glitter.

Available in stores and online!

ZONDERVAN®
.com

Let's Be Real

Living Life as an Open and Honest You

Natasha Bure

From singer, model, and YouTube celebrity Natasha Bure, the daughter of Candace Cameron Bure, comes a real, honest conversational book that doesn't hold back. Everywhere she goes and every video she posts has one basic message: this is real, this is life, and we all go through it. Whether it's acne, boyfriends, faith, stress, or having fun, Natasha's view is simply to be honest, simply to be real, no matter what you face. Natasha's real and relatable tone paired with personal notes and stories will help readers see that living a "real" life is the best life.

Let's Be Real features a stunning dust jacket with embossing and foil.

Available in stores and online!